PULL UP YOUR SOCKS!

PULL UP YOUR SOCKS!

JENNY OCCLESHAW

NEW
HOLLAND

This book is for my dear friend Caroline who does not knit socks but who has given me the inspiration to knit so many pairs of beautiful socks and has given me her support, strength and wisdom over many years of friendship. That is what socks and friends are for.

CONTENTS

INTRODUCTION

Have you always wanted to knit socks and been too afraid to try because in the past some patterns you have read seem very complicated. Do not despair. This is the book for you. From basic sock patterns for the whole family right up to the most challenging "Kaleidoscope Socks" comprised of knitted circle motifs. When you have built your confidence up there is a pair of socks in this book for every sock knitter and for every would be sock knitter.

Socks to me are like little miniature works of art. They start off as a tiny ring of stitches and with a little bit of knitting turn into a fully completed beautiful piece of footwear with no sewing up involved. They are a portable project which you can take on the train or on long car trips. Once you have mastered the basics you can start to add your own flourishes such as stripes and different ribbed patterns.

One of the best things of all is that there is the most spectacular range of sock yarns available. Every imaginable color in both fingering and worsted weight. Friends and family will love you forever if you bestow the gift of handmade socks upon them as not only is it a gift of love but the warmth and fit of a hand knitted pair of socks cannot be matched by anything machine made.

I wrote this book because I wanted knitters to experience the same joy I have in knitting socks and so that there is a book which gives patterns for the whole family. Please enjoy knitting your socks and if you are a new sock knitter do start off with one of the plainer pairs first. That way you will find you master all the basics and are ready for more intricate patterns.

Happy Sock Knitting!

Jenny Occleshaw

ESSENTIAL KNITTING TECHNIQUES

This section describes the techniques required to teach you how to knit. You'll need time and patience to learn and perfect the different techniques, but with practice and determination you'll soon master the basics. It is inevitable that you will make mistakes, but that is all part of the learning process. You'll find in no time at all that you'll be knitting projects for your family and yourself!

How to Cast On

To begin knitting, you will need to create a foundation row of stitches on your needle by "casting on."

1. Make a slipknot by looping yarn into a pretzel shape, leaving a tail end at least three times the width of what you are knitting (if your scarf is 20 cm (8 in) wide, you'll need a 60 cm (24-in) long tail). Slip knitting needle through pretzel shape, and pull yarn ends to tighten.
2. Drape tail of yarn over left thumb and working yarn (ball end) over left index finger. Use your other fingers to catch yarn lengths in left palm. Insert needle upward through the loop on your thumb.
3. With the needle, catch the working yarn that's on your index finger, and pull it through the loop on your thumb. Remove thumb from loop. Keeping yarn ends secured in palm, reposition thumb, and tighten new stitch on right-hand needle. Repeat these steps until you've cast on the required number of stitches.

The Knit Stitch

Now you have mastered casting on, you can begin to form the first of two fundamental movements in knitting, the *knit stitch* and the *purl stitch*. Knit stitch forms a flat, vertical loop on the fabric face.

1. Hold the needle with cast-on stitches in your left hand. Wrap the working yarn around your left index finger, and hold it back on the left-hand needle.
2. Insert point of right-hand needle from front to back into the first cast-on stitch on the left-hand needle, opening up a stitch.
3. Catch working yarn with right-hand needle.
4. Pull yarn through opened stitch.
5. Slip cast-on stitch off left-hand needle while holding middle finger against second cast-on stitch to ensure it does not also slip off. The stitch on the right-hand needle

is the newly formed knit stitch. Continue knitting across the cast-on row. When you have emptied the last stitch from the left-hand needle (completing a row), exchange needles, returning the needle with stitching to your left hand.

The Purl Stitch

The purl stitch is the other fundamental stitch used in knitting. When you use this stitch along with the knit stitch it will form stocking stitch. This will produce fabric which is flat and smooth on one side and has slightly raised lines on the other. Once you have learned and mastered these two techniques, the stitches will form the basis for a huge range of patterns.

The purl stitch differs from the knit stitch in two fundamental ways: The working yarn is held in the front of the project instead of the back, and the needle is inserted from the back to the front instead of from front to back.

1. Hold the needle with cast-on stitches in your left hand. Wrap the working yarn (ball end) around your left index finger, and hold it in front of the work.
2. Insert point of right-hand needle, from back to front, into the first cast-on stitch on the left-hand needle, opening up a stitch.
3. Lay working yarn over needle from front to back by moving left index finger downward.
4. Push working yarn from front to back through cast-on stitch. Slip cast-on stitch off left-hand needle while holding middle finger against second cast-on stitch to ensure it does not also slip off. The stitch on the right-hand needle is the newly formed purl stitch. As a purl stitch faces you, it looks like a grain of rice; its reverse side looks like a V.

How to Cast Off

These necessary steps keep stitches from unravelling once they are removed from the needle.

1. Knit two stitches. Insert left-hand needle into first stitch; lift stitch up over second stitch and off the needle. Continue knitting stitches in this manner until all stitches have been cast off. Cut working yarn, leaving a 15 cm (6-inch) long tail. Pull tail through last stitch to secure.
2. Use a yarn needle to weave tail ends of yarn through backs of several stitches, picking up only surface loops.

Knitting On a Set of 4 Needles (Knitting in the Round)

Many beginner knitters are intimidated by the process of knitting in the round because of the double-sided needles used to carry out this skill. However, as long as you know how to knit with two needles, it's really not that difficult – and then you will be able to create sweaters, hats, socks, and more, all with even seams.

You will need four double-pointed needles.

1. Cast your stitches onto 1 needle only. Divide the stitches evenly among 3 needles by slipping them onto 2 more needles.

2. Once all 3 needles have the same number of stitches, lay the needles flat on a table, loosely lined up end to end. (Your right-most needle should have the working yarn.) Make sure stitches aren't twisted; they should all face the same direction.

3. Join the needles to form a triangle as follows: Take the left needle in your left hand and the right needle in your right hand. Bring the needles together to form a triangle with the middle needle. Pick up your fourth needle. With the triangle still in place (and the working yarn on the right needle), knit the stitches onto the left needle, pulling working yarn tightly to join (see the image below). You are now knitting in the round.

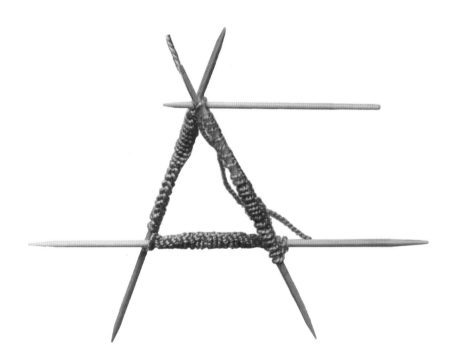

Working From a Chart

Colored patterns and designs are often charted on graph paper and make it much easier for the knitter to follow. Each square on the chart represents a stitch and each horizontal line of squares represents rows of stitches. Charts can be either colored or just black and white and they will always have a key at the side with different symbols depicting the different shades. You will read charts from bottom to top and normally from right to left. They are usually in stocking stitch and odd-numbered rows will be knit and even numbered rows will be purl, the first stitch of a chart being the bottom one on the right. Placing a straight edge of some kind, like a ruler or piece of card under each row will help you keep your place in the chart when working the design.

Tension

Tension is the resistance on the yarn as it passes through the fingers that are controlling it. Consistent, correct and exact tension is what every novice knitter is striving to achieve. Tension is THE most important thing with any garment you are going to make. This will determine the finished size of your garment, whether it fits you or is far too small or too big.

Your tension and the tension specified in the pattern must be the same so that your project will be the correct size. Before starting your project, take the time to make a tension swatch.

To check tension, using the same yarn, needles and pattern stitch specified in the instructions, make a swatch that is approximately 15 cm (6 in) square. Work in pattern for about 15 cm (6 in), and then bind off.

Let the swatch relax for a bit, and then flatten it without stretching to measure. Using pins, mark off a section of stitches in the center of the swatch that measures 10 cm (4 in) square. Count the number of stitches and rows in this 10 cm (4 in) section. If they match the tension, you can start right in on your pattern

FINISHING AND MAKING UP

Grafting

This technique is frequently used to close the toe of socks or the tips of mittens. This is an excellent way of invisibly joining two pieces of knitting. The edges are not cast off and the knitting can be joined either while it is still on the needles or after it has been taken off.

Grafting with Knitting on the Needles

- Thread a wool or tapestry needle with a length of knitting yarn. Place the two pieces to be joined with right sides facing and hold the knitting needles in the left hand.
- *Pass the wool needle knit-wise through the first stitch on the front needle and slip the stitch off the knitting needle. Pass the wool needle purl-wise through the second stitch on the same needle, leaving the stitch on the needle. Pass purl-wise through the first stitch on the back knitting needle and slip the stitch off, then pass knit-wise through the second stitch on the same needle, leaving the stitch on the needle. Repeat from*.

KNITTING TERMINOLOGY

When following a knitting pattern you will find that the instructions contain a special vocabulary, much of it is abbreviated. It can be a little confusing when you first begin to read patterns but you will soon get to learn the different meanings. I have listed below the most common terms and their meanings. When using the patterns in this book you will refer to them. On some patterns there are special abbreviations needed but these are listed on the instructions for that particular design.

Abbreviations

K = knit
P = purl
St st = stocking stitch (USA Stockinet Stitch)
Cast Off. (USA Bind Off)
K2tog = knit 2 stitches together, thus decreasing a stitch
P2tog = purl 2 stitches together, thus decreasing a stitch
Tbl = through back of loop
Alt = alternate
Beg = beginning
Inc = increase
Dec = decrease
Rep = repeat.
Sts = stitches
Sl = slip
Ssk = slip 2 sts on to the right hand needle and knit together
Patt = pattern
Psso = pass slipped stitch over
Yfwd = yarn forward, bringing yarn to front of work between the
  two needles, this creates a stitch
Yrn = yarn round needle.
Yo = yarn over needle.
M1 = make 1, pick up the loop which lies between the two needles
  and knit into the back of it, place on right hand needle
RS = right side of work
WS = wrong side of work

Projects

FIRST SOCKS

Socks make a great gift for new Mothers. They are much more useful than booties and easier to knit. They are quick and you can use up all your bits and pieces of 4 ply and be quite creative once you have knitted a couple of pairs.

SKILL LEVEL
Basic knitting skills

SIZE
Baby aged – 6–9 months

TENSION
38sts and 48 rows to 10cm (4in) of stocking st worked on 2.25mm (UK 13, US 1) double pointed knitting needles.

Be sure to measure tension carefully. If less sts try use one size smaller needles. If more sts try using one size larger needles.

MATERIALS
Yarn:
- 1 x 50 g (2 oz) ball of 4 ply variegated Pink yarn. (You will not need the whole ball).

Knitting Needles:
- 1 set of 4, 2.25mm (UK 13, US 1) double pointed knitting needles
- Wool needle for sewing up and grafting toe.

Socks

(Make 2)

Using a set of 4, 2.25mm (UK 13, US 1) double pointed knitting needles and Pink 4 ply cast on 48 sts…16,16,16.

Work in K1, P1 Rib for 5cm (2in).

Change to Stocking st. Work in Stocking st (Knit every round) for 4cm (1½ in)

Commence Heel

Slip 8 sts from end of second needle on to beginning of third needle. These 24 sts are for the heel. Divide rem sts between 2 needles for instep.

Note – Heel is worked backwards and forwards in rows on two needles.

1st row – Sl 1, Purl to end of row.

2nd row – Sl 1, Knit to end of row.

Rep these 2 rows 6 times then 1st row once.

Turn heel

Next row – K13 , K1, Sl 1, K1, psso, K1, turn, P4, P2tog, P1, turn, K5, Sl 1, K1, psso, k1, turn, P6, P2tog, P1, turn, K7, Sl 1, K1, psso. K1, turn, cont in this manner until all sts are worked on to one needle and 14 sts rem. Knit back 7 sts. Slip all instep sts back on to one needle…24 sts.

Shape Instep

Taking an empty needle knit rem 7 sts of heel and knit up 8 sts along side of heel. With second needle knit across instep sts; with third needle knit up 8 sts along other side of heel and rem 7 heel sts.

1st round – Knit.

2nd round – First needle – Knit to last 3 sts K2tog, K1; Second needle – Knit; Third needle – K1, Sl 1, psso. Knit to end.

Rep these 2 rounds until 12 sts rem on needle 1 and 3 and 24 sts rem on needle 2. Work a further 12 rounds without shaping.

Shape Toe

1st round – First needle – Knit to last 3 sts, K2tog, K1; Second needle – K1, Sl 1, K1, psso, knit to last 3 sts, K2tog, K1; Third needle – K1, Sl 1, K1, psso. Knit to end.

2nd round – Knit.

Rep these 2 rounds until 4 sts rem on needle one and 3 and 8 sts rem on needle two. Knit one round and then first needle of next round. Slip sts from third needle on to end of first needle thus completing the round.

Toe is now ready for grafting (refer to page 12 for instructions). Darn in any loose ends. Press lightly if needed.

COSY TOES

These gorgeous little booties are sure to be a hit with new Mothers. The ribbon ties will help keep them securely in place. They are knitted in pure baby Alpaca giving them the softest feel. Two sizes are given and 2, 50 g (2 oz) balls will easily make you a couple of pairs.

SKILL LEVEL
Basic knitting skills

SIZE
Baby aged: 6–12 months
Toddler aged: 18 months – 2 years

TENSION
24 sts and 40 rows to 10cm (4in) measured over st st on 2.75mm (UK 13, US 1) knitting needles.

MATERIALS
For each pair
Yarn:
- 1 x 50 g (2 oz) ball Blue Sky Baby Alpaca Sport weight
- 1 x 50 g (2 oz) ball Royal Blue Baby Alpaca Sport weight (for contrast) small amount only is needed. Sport weight is equivalent to approx 5 ply
- Colors used
- 536 – Green
- 535 – Blue
- 538 – Pink
- 521 – Orange

Knitting Needle:
- 1 pair of 2.75mm (UK 13, US 1) knitting needles
- Wool needle for sewing up

Extras:
- 2 felt flowers for each pair of booties
- 1 metre of 5cm (2in) satin ribbon
- Polyester sewing cotton
- Sewing needle

Booties
(make 2)
Note – The booties have a seam at the back of the heel and under the foot.
Using 2.75mm (UK 13, US 1) knitting needles and Blue Sky Baby Alpaca in main color, cast on 37, (43) sts.
1st row – Knit.
2nd row – K2, m1, K16, (19), m1, K1, m1,

K16, (K19), m1, K1, p1.

3rd row – Knit.

4th row – K3, m1, K16, (19), m1, K3, m1, K16, (19), m1, K2, p1.

5th row – Knit.

6th row – K4, m1, K16, (19), m1, K5, m1, K16, (19), m1, K3, p1.

7th row – Knit.

8th row – K5, m1, K16, (19), m1, K5, m1, K16, (19), m1, K4, p1.

9th row – Knit.

10th row – K6, m1, K16, (19), m1, K9, m1, K16, (19), m1, K5, p1.

11th row – Knit.

12th row – Purl.

13th row – Knit...56 (62 sts).

14th, 15th, 16th and 17th rows – Work 4 rows garter st without further shaping.

18th, 19th, 20th, 21st, 22nd, 23rd and 24th rows – Beg with a purl row work 7 rows st st..

Top shaping

Next row

25th row – K20, (21) SSKx4(5) times, K1, K2tog x4(5)times K19(20, p1.

26th row – K1, purl to end of row.

27th row – K18,(20), SSK x 3(3)times, K1, Ktog, K2tog x3, (3) times, K17, (19),p1.

28th row – K1, purl to end.

29th row – K15, (17), SSK x3 (3)times, K1, K2tog, K2tog x 3, (3)tims, K14,16, p1.

30th row – Change to contrast color and Purl 3 rows (for both sizes).

31st to 34th row – K2 *, yfwd, K2tog, rep from * to last st, K1. (picot row)

Begin with a purl row work 3 rows st st (both sizes).

Cast off.

To Make Up

With right sides together and using a mattress seam or fine back stitch seam, sew heel and sole seam. Fold the top edging to the inside at the picot row and stitch to the first row of the color change. Ensure that you don't pull this stitching too tightly. Darn in any loose ends.

Turn to the right side. Cut ribbon to the desired length and commencing at centre front, thread through the holes created by the picot row all the way around the top edge and tie in a bow at the centre front.

Stitch the felt flower in place on the toe using polyester cotton and sewing needle. If preferred, you could make a small crochet flower in matching yarn or use a little pompom.

CHRISTMAS SOCKS

Socks make great Christmas presents. These dear little socks have a roll top made from soft white Angora yarn. These will also make great little tree decorations if you sew a ribbon loop on the back of them. You can even pop a little gift in them. These are baby size socks.

SKILL LEVEL
Basic knitting skills

SIZE
Baby aged – 6–9 months

TENSION
38 sts and 48 rows to 10cm (4in) of stocking st worked on 2.25mm (UK 13, US 1) double pointed knitting needles.
Be sure to measure tension carefully. If less sts try using one size smaller needles. If more sts try using one size larger needles.

MATERIALS
Yarn:
- 1 x 50 g (2 oz) ball, 4 ply Red Sock Yarn.
- Small amount of 4 ply White Angora Yarn. (Mohair would be a suitable alternative)

Knitting Needles:
- 1 set of 4, 2.25mm (UK 13, US 1) double pointed knitting needles.
- Wool needle for grafting toe and darning in ends.

Socks
(Make 2)
Using the double pointed knitting needles, and 4 ply White Angora, cast on 48 sts…16,16,16. Join into a round being careful not to twist stitches.
Work 7 rounds st st.
Change to Red 4 ply. Break of White Angora.
Work 1 round st st. Change to K1, P1 rib. Work in rib for 5cm (2in). Change to st st. Work in st st for 4cm (1½ in).

Commence Heel
Slip 8 sts from end of second needle on to beginning of third needle. These 24 sts are for heel. Divide rem sts between 2 needles for instep.
Note – Heel is worked backwards and forwards in rows on two needles.

1st row – Sl 1, Purl to end of row.

2nd row – Sl 1, Knit to end of row.

Rep these 2 rows 6 times then 1st row once.

Turn heel.

Next row – K13, K1, Sl 1, K1, psso, K1, turn, P4, P2tog, P1, turn, K5, Sl 1, K1, psso, k1, turn, P6, P2tog, P1, turn, K7, Sl 1, K1, psso. K1, turn, cont in this manner until all sts are worked on to one needle and 14 sts rem. Knit back 7 sts. Slip all instep sts back on to one needle…24 sts.

Shape Instep

Taking an empty needle knit rem 7 sts of heel and knit up 8 sts along side of heel. With second needle knit across instep sts; with third needle knit up 8 sts along other side of heel and rem 7 heel sts.

1st round – Knit.

2nd round – First needle – Knit to last 3 sts K2tog, K1; Second needle – Knit; Third needle – K1, Sl 1, psso. Knit to end.

Rep these 2 rounds until 12 sts rem on needle one and three and 24 sts rem on needle two. Work a further 12 rounds without shaping.

Shape Toe

1st round – First needle – Knit to last 3 sts, K2tog, K1; Second needle – K1, Sl 1, K1, psso, knit to last 3 sts, K2tog, K1; Third needle – K1, Sl 1, K1, psso. Knit to end.

2nd round – Knit.

Rep these 2 rounds until 4 sts rem on

needle one and three and 8 sts rem on needle two. Knit one round and then first needle of next round. Slip sts from third needle on to end of first needle thus completing the round.

Toe is now ready for grafting (refer to page 12 for instructions). Darn in any loose ends. Press lightly if needed.

RUFFLES

The addition of the mohair ruffle turns a plain sock into something very special. I used Rowan Kid Silk Mohair but any fine gauge mohair would be suitable. Work the ruffle of two straight needles first as you will have a lot of stitches to cope with and then swap on to a set of four when you are ready to commence the rib.

SKILL LEVEL
Intermediate knitting skills

SIZE
Baby aged – 6–9 months

TENSION
38 sts and 48 rows to 10cm (4in) of stocking st worked on 2.25mm (UK 13, US 1) double pointed knitting needles.

Measure tension carefully. If less sts try using one size smaller needles. If more sts try using one size larger needles.

MATERIALS
Yarn:
- 1 x 50 g (2 oz) ball of 4 ply, Bright Blue sock yarn.
- Small amount of Navy Rowan Kid Silk Haze

Knitting Needles:
- 1 pair of 2.75mm (UK 12, US) knitting needles

- 1 set of 4, 2.25mm (UK 13, US 1) double pointed knitting needles.
- Wool needle for sewing up and grafting toe.

Ruffle and sock

Using 2.75mm (UK 12, US) knitting needles and Rowan Kid Silk Haze, cast on 192 sts. Knit one row.

Next row – K2tog all across…96 sts.

Next row – K2tog all across…48 sts.
Knit one row.

Divide sts on to a set of 4…16,16,16. (Change to Bright Blue 4 ply Sock Wool and commence sock).

Work in K1, P1 Rib for 8cm (3¼in).

Change to Stocking st. Work in Stocking st (Knit every round) for 2cm (¾in)

Commence Heel

Slip 8 sts from end of second needle on to beginning of third needle. These 24 sts are for the heel. Divide rem sts between two needles for instep.

Note – Heel is worked backwards and forwards in rows on two needles.

1st row – Sl 1, Purl to end of row.

2nd row – Sl 1, Knit to end of row.

Rep these 2 rows 6 times then 1st row once.

Turn heel

Next row – K13, K1, Sl 1, K1, psso, K1, turn, P4, P2tog, P1, turn, K5, Sl 1, K1, psso, k1, turn, P6, P2tog, P1, turn, K7, Sl 1, K1, psso. K1, turn, cont in this manner until all sts are worked on to one needle and 14 sts rem. Knit back 7 sts. Slip all instep sts back on to one needle…24 sts.

Shape Instep

Taking an empty needle knit rem 7 sts of heel and knit up 8 sts along side of heel. With second needle knit across instep sts; with third needle knit up 8 sts along other side of heel and rem 7 heel sts.

1st round – Knit.

2nd round – First needle – Knit to last 3 sts K2tog, K1; Second needle – Knit; Third needle K1, Sl 1, psso. Knit to end.

Rep these 2 rounds until 12 sts rem on needle one and three and 24 sts rem on needle two.

Work a further 12 rounds without shaping.

Shape Toe

1st round – First needle – Knit to last 3 sts, K2tog, K1; Second needle – K1, Sl 1, K1, psso, knit to last 3 sts, K2tog, K1; Third needle – K1, Sl 1, K1, psso, Knit to end.

2nd round – Knit.

Rep these 2 rounds until 4 sts rem on needle one and three and 8 sts rem on needle two. Knit one round and then first needle of next round. Slip sts from third needle on to end of first needle thus completing the round.

Toe is now ready for grafting (refer to page 12 for instructions). Darn in any loose ends. Press lightly if needed.

LITTLE SMARTIE SOCKS

These socks, for the little person in your life, look like they have little Smarties around the ankle. Once you have mastered your basic sock technique they are not difficult to do. They are great for using up little odds and ends of yarn and make perfect gifts. Everyone loves being given a lovely pair of socks and these ones are very special.

SKILL LEVEL
Advanced knitting skills

SIZE
Baby aged – 6-9 months

TENSION
38 sts and 48 rows to 10cm (4in) of stocking st worked on 2.25mm (UK 13, US 1) double pointed knitting needles.

Be sure to measure tension carefully. If less sts try using one size smaller needles. If more sts try using one size larger needles.

SPECIAL ABBREVIATION
MB – Make Bobble. (Bobble is worked thus – K1, p1, k1, p1, k1 into same st, (5 sts) turn, purl, turn knit, turn purl, turn, knit, *pass second st on needle over the first, rep from * until one st rem.)

MATERIALS
Yarn:
- 1 x 50 g (2 oz) ball of 4 ply, Jade Green
- Small amount of 4 ply, Dark pink
- Small amount of 4 ply, Bright Pink
- Small amount of 4 ply, Light Blue
- Small amount of 4 ply, Royal blue

Knitting Needles:
- 1 set of 4, 2.25mm (UK 13, US 1) double pointed knitting needles.
- Wool needle for grafting toe and darning in ends.
- 1, 2.25mm (UK 13, US 1) knitting needle for holding loops.

Socks
Using a set of 4, 2.25mm (UK 13, US 1) double pointed knitting needles and 4 ply Jade Green, cast on 48 sts… 16,16,16. Join into a ring being careful

not to twist sts. Work in K2, P2 rib for 5cm (2in).

Change to stocking st, (every round knit). Increase 2 sts on first round…50 sts.

Work a further 2 rounds st st.

First bobble round – Choose Bobble color – *K4, MB, rep from * to last st, MB.

Work 5 round st st.

Second bobble round – Use second Bobble color – K2,*MB, K4, rep from *, to last 2 sts, K2.

Work 5 round st st.

Third bobble round – As for first bobble round.

Work a further 10 rounds st st, dec 2 sts on last round… 48 sts.

Commence Heel

Slip 8 sts from end of second needle on to beginning of third needle. These 24 sts are for the heel. Divide rem sts between 2 needles for instep.

Note – Heel is worked backwards and forwards in rows on two needles.

1st row – Sl 1, Purl to end of row.

2nd row – Sl 1, Knit to end of row.

Rep these 2 rows 6 times then 1st row once.

Turn heel

Next row – K13, K1, Sl 1, K1, psso, K1, turn, P4, P2tog, P1, turn, K5, Sl 1, K1, k1, turn, P6, P2tog, P1, turn, K7, Sl 1, K1, psso. K1, turn. Cont in this manner until all sts are worked on to one needle and 14 sts rem. Knit back 7 sts. Slip all instep sts back on to one needle… 24 sts.

Shape Instep

Taking an empty needle knit rem 7 sts of heel and knit up 8 sts along side of heel. With second needle knit across instep sts; with third needle knit up 8 sts along other side of heel and rem 7 heel sts.

1st round – Knit.

2nd round – First needle – knit to last 3 sts K2tog, K1; Second needle – Knit; Third needle – K1, Sl 1, psso. Knit to end.

Rep these 2 rounds until 12 sts rem on

needle one and three and 24 sts rem on needle teo. Work a further 12 rounds without shaping.

Contrast Stripe

For Pink Bobble Sock – Work 1 round Royal Blue, 1 Round Light Blue, I round Royal Blue.

For Blue Bobble Sock – Work 1 round Light Pink, I round Dark Pink, I Round Light Pink.

Shape Toe

1st round – First needle – Knit to last 3 sts, K2tog, K1; Second needle – K1, Sl 1, K1, psso, knit to last 3 sts, K2tog, K1; Third needle – K1, Sl 1, K1, psso. Knit to end.

2nd round – Knit.

Rep these 2 rounds until 4 sts rem on needle one and three and 8 sts rem on needle two. Knit one round and then first needle of next round. Slip sts from third needle on to end of first needle thus completing the round.

Toe is now ready for grafting (refer to page 12 for instructions). Darn in any loose ends. Press lightly if needed.

LOOPY TWIRLY SOCKS

Once you have got the hang of basic sock knitting you might want to try your hand at a few variations. These loopy socks will brighten up a plain outfit for your little toddler as well as keeping their feet warm. Make all the loops first and keep them on a spare needle and then just knit them in as you go. The result is quite amazing.

SKILL LEVEL
Advanced knitting skills

SIZE
Baby aged – 6–9 months
(Length of foot and leg can be lengthened, however, bear in mind you will need extra yarn)

TENSION
38 sts and 48 rows to 10cm (4in) of stocking st worked on 2.25mm (UK 13, US 1) double pointed knitting needles.
Be sure to measure tension carefully. If less sts try using one size smaller needles. If more sts try using one size larger needles.

MATERIALS
Yarn:
- 1 x 50 g (2 oz) ball of 4 ply, Bright Pink sock yarn
- Small amount of 4 ply, Dark Pink
- Small amount of 4 ply, Jade Green
- Small amount of 4 ply, Light Blue
- Small amount of 4 ply, Royal Blue

Knitting Needles:
- 1 set of 4, 2.25mm (UK 13, US 1) double pointed knitting needles.
- Wool needle for grafting toe and darning in ends.
- 1, 2.25 (UK 13, US 1) knitting needle for holding loops.

Loops
(Make 24 for each sock)
Make 6 loops of each of the 4 colors.Once the loops are made place them on the spare knitting needle keeping them in the same order - i.e. pink, green, light blue, royal blue, pink, green, Light blue, royal blue).
Using 2, 2.25mm (UK 13, US 1) double

pointed knitting needles and 4 ply, cast on 20 sts.

Next row – Cast off 19 sts. Pick up a loop at the beg of the cast on end. Place it on the right hand needle and knit it. Pass the second st on the right hand needle over the first st. Place the completed loop on the spare needle.

Make another 23 loops.

Socks

(Make 2)

Note – Work the toe color in contrasting shades i.e. one in Jade Green, one in Royal Blue.

Using a set of 4, 2.25mm (UK 13, US 1) double pointed knitting needles and Pink 4 ply, cast on 48 sts…16,16,16. Join into a ring being careful not to twist sts.

Work 10 rounds of stocking st (every round knit). Change to K1, P1 rib and work 3 rounds.

Next round – Insert loops – * Slip loop off the spare needle on to working needle and Knit together with next st, Rib 3, rep from * to end of round.

Work 5 rounds K1, P1 rib.

Next round – Rib 2, * Slip loop off the spare needle on to working needle and Knit together with next st, Rib 3, rep from * to last st, P1.

Work 5 round K1, P1, rib.

Work 4cm (1½in) Stocking st.

Commence Heel

Slip 8 sts from end of second needle on to beginning of third needle. These 24 sts are for the heel. Divide rem sts between 2 needles for instep.

Note – Heel is worked backwards and forwards in rows on two needles.

1st row – Sl 1, Purl to end of row.

2nd row – Sl 1, Knit to end of row.

Rep these 2 rows 6 times then 1st row once.

Turn heel

Next row – K13, K1, Sl 1, K1, psso, K1, turn, P4, P2tog, P1, turn, K5, Sl 1, K1, psso, k1, turn, P6, P2tog, P1, turn, K7, Sl 1, K1, psso. K1, turn, cont in this manner until all sts are worked on to one needle and 14 sts rem. Knit back 7 sts. Slip all instep sts back on to one needle…24 sts

Shape Instep

Taking an empty needle knit rem 7 sts of heel and knit up 8 sts along side of heel. With second needle knit across instep sts; with third needle knit up 8 sts along other side of heel and rem 7 heel sts.

1st round – Knit.

2nd round – First needle – Knit to last 3 sts K2tog, K1; Second needle – Knit; Third needle – K1, Sl 1, psso. Knit to end.

Rep these 2 rounds until 12 sts rem on needle one and three and 24 sts rem on needle two. Work a further 12 rounds without shaping.

Shape Toe

Change to contrasting color (choose one
of the colors from the loops)

1st round – First needle – Knit to last 3 sts,
K2tog, K1; Second needle – K1, Sl 1, K1,
psso, knit to last 3 sts, K2tog, K1; Third
needle – K1, Sl 1, K1, psso. Knit to end.

2nd round – Knit.

Rep these 2 rounds until 4 sts rem on
needle one and three and 8 sts rem on
needle two. Knit one round and then first
needle of next round. Slip sts from third
needle on to end of first needle thus
completing the round.

Toe is now ready for grafting (refer to page
12 for instructions). Darn in any loose
ends. Press lightly if needed.

ODDS AND ENDS BABY SLIPPERS

When you knit socks you invariably end up with all sorts of little bits of odds and ends of wool left over. This pattern is great for using up those bits and pieces. The slippers fit a really little baby and are very sweet. You can add a ribbon at the heel if you want to make ties. They make an excellent gift for new mothers or a great addition to the school fete.

Once you get going you can make a pair in an evening.

SKILL LEVEL
Advanced knitting skills

SIZE
Small baby foot – 7cm (2¾in) long

TENSION
47.5 sts to 10cm in width measured over garter st on 2.25mm (UK 13, US 1) double pointed knitting needles.

MATERIALS
Yarn:
- 25 g (1 oz) of 4 ply, sock wool (only a small amount of yarn is needed for this project).

Knitting Needles:
- 1 set of 4, 2.25mm (UK 13, US 1) double pointed knitting needles.
- Wool needle for darning in ends.

Extras:
- 2 x 1.5cm (¾in) Felt balls
- Sewing needle
- Matching polyester sewing thread

Slippers
(Make 2)
Using 2, 2.25mm (UK 13, US 1) double pointed knitting needles and 4 ply yarn, cast on 7 sts.
1st row – Knit.
2nd row – Knit.
3rd row – K1, inc in next st, knit to last 3 sts, inc in next st, K2.
4th row – Knit.
Rep rows 3 and 4 until there are 15 sts.
Cont in garter st (every row knit) until work measures 6.5cm (2½in).
Next row – K1, K2tog, Knit to last 3 sts, K2tog, K1.
Next row – Knit.

Rep these last 2 rows until 5 sts rem.
This completes the sole.

With 5 sts on the needle, pick up and
knit 28 sts down first side of foot to the
centre of the toe onto the same needle.
Take another needle and pick up and knit
29 sts along other side of foot, ending at
the 5 original sts. Slip the original 5 sts
on to a third needle…28,5,29 (the centre
st of the 5 is the beginning of the round).

Round 1 – Purl.
Round 2 – K25, K2tog, K8, Sl 1, K1, psso,
K25.
Round 3 – Purl.
Round 4 – K24, K2tog, K8, Sl 1, K1, psso,
K24.
Round 5 – Purl.
Round 6 – K23, K2tog, K8, Sl 1, K1, psso,
K23.
Round 7 – Purl.
Round 8 – K22, K2tog, K8, Sl 1, K1, psso,
K22.
Round 9 – Purl.
Round 10 – K21, (K2tog) 3 times, (Sl !, K1,
psso) 3 times K21.
Round 11 – Purl.
Round 12 – K18, (K2tog) 3 times, (Sl !, K1,
psso)3 times K18.
Round 13 – Purl.
Round 14 – K15, (K2tog) 3 times, (Sl !, K1,
psso)3 times K15.
Round 15 – Purl.
Cast off.

Darn in loose ends. Make another slipper
to match. Stitch felt balls to tops of toes.

BLUE HUES

This is a great pair of socks for the bushwalking or gardening family. They are for the older child and will fit well into boots or shoes and will keep feet warm in the colder weather. Sock wool is machine washable. Just don't put it in the tumble dryer or you will have socks for little tiny mice.

SKILL LEVEL
Basic knitting skills

SIZE
Girls medium foot (UK 10–11, EUR 28–39, US 10.5–11.5)

TENSION
35 sts and 40 rows to 10cm (4in) in width over stocking st worked on 2.25mm (UK 13, US 1) double pointed knitting needles.

Be sure to measure tension carefully. If less sts try using one size smaller needles. If more sts try using one size larger needles.

MATERIALS
Yarn:
- 1 x 100 g (3½ oz) hank of 4 ply, Rowan Fine Art in aqua blue shades.
- Any 4 ply sock yarn is a suitable alternative.

Knitting Needles:
- 1 set of 4, 2.25mm (UK 13, US 1) double pointed knitting needles.
- Wool needle for grafting toe and darning in ends.

Socks
(Make 2)

Using a set of 4, 2.25mm (UK 13, US 1) double pointed knitting needles and 4 ply Rowan Fine Art, cast on 60 sts… 20,20,20. Join into a ring being careful not to twist sts.

Work in K2, P2 Rib for 10cm (4in).

Change to Stocking Stitch (every round knit) for 5cm (2in).

Divide for Heel

Knit first 15 sts of round on to one needle. Slip the last 15 sts of round on to the end of the same needle. These are the heel sts. Divide rem sts between two needles and leave for instep.

Note – Heel is worked backwards and

forwards in rows on two needles

1st row – Sl 1, Purl to end.

2nd row – *Sl 1, K1, rep from* to last st, K1.
Rep these 2 rows 12 times and then 1st
    row once.

Turn Heel

Knit 17, Sl 1, K1, psso, K1, turn, P6, P2tog,
    P1, turn, K7, Sl 1, K1, psso, K1, turn,
    P8, P2tog, P1, K9, Sl 1, K1, psso, K1,
    turn, cont in this manner until all sts are
    worked on to one needle…18 sts. Knit
    back first 9 sts. Heel is now complete.
    Slip all instep sts back on to one needle.

Shape Foot

First needle – Knit 9 heel sts, pick up and
    knit 16 sts along first side of heel; Second
    needle – Knit across instep sts; Third
    needle – Pick up and knit 16 sts along
    other side of heel knit rem 9 heel sts.
    Knitting is now back in the round.

Decrease for instep

1st round – Knit.

2nd round – First needle – Knit to last
    4 sts, K2tog, K2; Second needle – Knit;
    Third needle – K2, Sl 1, K1, psso. Knit to
    end.
Rep these two rounds until 15 sts rem on
    needle one and three and 30 sts rem on
    needle two. Cont in stocking st without
    further shaping until work measures
    15cm (6in) from where sts were picked up
    at side of heel.

Toe Shaping

1st round – Knit.

2nd round – First needle – Knit to last 4
    sts, K2tog, K2; Second needle – K2, K1,
    Sl 1, psso K to last 4 sts K2tog, K2; Third
    needle – K2, Sl 1, K1, psso. Knit to end.
Rep these 2 rounds until 7 sts rem on
    needle one and three and 14 sts rem on
    needle two. Slip sts from third needle on
    to end of first needle thus completing
    the round.

Toe is now ready for grafting (refer to page
    12 for instructions). Darn in any loose
    ends. Press lightly if needed.

BUBBLEGUM RIBBED SOCKS

These calf length socks are knitted in a rib pattern which is great for staying up on little legs. They are suitable for a child's foot approximately 15cm (6in). The leg and foot length can be altered but be aware that you may need more yarn. Knit these for a six or seven-year-old.

I have knitted them in a beautiful "Koigu" KPPPM Hand painted Merino yarn. This yarn does need to be hand washed so bear this in mind if you are not a keen hand washer of socks and use an alternate yarn to achieve the same tension.

SKILL LEVEL
Basic knitting skills

SIZE
Girl's small foot (UK 7.5, EU 25.5, US 8)

TENSION
36 sts and 42 rows to 10cm (4in) of stocking st worked on 2.25mm (UK 13, US 1) knitting needles.

Correct tension is important. Be sure to measure tension carefully. If less sts try using one size smaller needles. If more sts try using one size larger needles.

MATERIALS
Yarn:
- 2 x 50 g (2 oz) balls of Koigu KPPM Merino Yarn, shade 3227.

Knitting Needles:
- 1 set of 4, 2.25mm (UK 13, US 1) double pointed knitting needles.
- Wool needle for grafting toe.

Socks

(Make 2)

Using a set of 4, 2.25mm (UK 13, US 1) double pointed knitting needles and Koigu yarn, cast on 56 sts…21,14,21.

Join into a ring being careful not to twist stitches.

Work in K1, P1 Rib for 4cm (1½in)

Commence Rib Patt

1st round – *K4, P3, rep from* to end of round.

2nd round – Knit.

Rep these two rounds until work measures 13cm (5in) from cast on edge.

Divide for Heel

Note – Heel is worked backwards and forwards in rows.

Next row – K14, slip last 14 sts from needle three onto same needle… 28 sts.

Divide rem sts between two needles and leave for instep.

1st row – Sl 1, Purl to end.

2nd row – * Sl 1, K1, rep from* to last st K1.

Rep the last 2 rows 6 times and then 1st row once.

Turn Heel – K17, turn, P6, turn, K5, Sl 1, K1, psso, K1, turn, P6, P2tog, P1, turn, K7, Sl 1, K1, psso, K1, turn, P8, P2tog, P1, turn, cont in this manner until all sts are worked on to one needle…16 sts.

Knit back 8 sts – Place all instep sts back on one needle.

Commencing at centre back of heel, K8, pick up and Knit 12 sts along side of heel. With next needle part in Rib across instep sts. With next needle pick up and knit 12 sts along other side of heel, knit rem 8 heel sts. Knitting is now back in the round.

Shape Instep.

1st round – Knit.

2nd round – First needle – Knit to last 4 sts, K2tog, K2; Second needle – Knit; Third needle – K2, Sl 1, K1, paso. Knit to end.

Rep these two rounds until 14 sts rem on needle one and three and 28 sts rem on needle two.

Cont without further shaping until foot measures 8cm (3¼ in) from where sts were picked up at side of heel.

Shape Toe.

1st round – Knit.

2nd round – First needle – Knit to last 4 sts, K2tog, K2; Second needle – K2, Sl 1, K1, psso, Kto last 4sts, K2tog, K2; Third needle – K2, Sl 1, K1, paso, knit to end.

Rep these 2 rows until 6 sts rem on needle one and three and 12 sts rem on needle two. Knit one more round, finishing by knitting all the stitches from needle one on to needle three.

Toe is now ready for grafting (refer to page 12 for instructions).

42

BASIC ANKLETS

Don't be put off trying your hand at knitting socks. There are so many fantastic sock yarns these days that the socks practically knit themselves. Socks have three parts, the cuff, the heel and the foot. If you have never knitted a sock before, try these first as I have designed them to make them as straight forward as possible. Once you have worn your own hand knitted pair of socks you will never look back.

SKILL LEVEL
Basic knitting skills

SIZE
Ladies small to medium foot (UK 5–8, EUR 38–42, US 7.5–10.5)
Length can be adjusted

TENSION
35 sts and 40 rows to 10cm (4in) in width over stocking st worked on 2.25mm (UK 13, US 1) double pointed knitting needles.
  Measure tension carefully. If less sts try using one size smaller needles. If more sts, try using one size larger needles.

MATERIALS
Yarn:
- 1 x 100 g (3½ oz) ball of 4 ply, Loopy Ewe Variegated sock yarn. This yarn comes with a separate ball of yarn for the heel and toe. Any 4 ply sock yarn is a suitable alternative.
- Loopy Ewe Yarn is 80% Merino and 20% Nylon. Perfect for socks and machine washable.

Knitting Needles:
- 1 set of 4, 2.25mm (UK 13, US 1) double pointed knitting needles.
- Wool needle for darning in ends.

Socks
(Make 2)
Using a set of 4, 2.25mm (UK 13, US 1) double pointed knitting needles and 4 Ply Loopy Ewe variegated yarn cast on 60 sts…20,20,20. Join in a ring being careful not to twist sts.
Work in K2, P2 rib for 13cm (5in).
Change to stocking stitch (every round knit). Work 10 rounds.

Divide for Heel

Break off variegated yarn and change to pale pink (or color of choice).

Knit first 15 sts of round on to one needle. Slip the last 15 sts of round on to the end of the same needle. These are the heel sts. Divide rem sts between 2 needles and leave for instep.

Note - Heel is worked backwards and forwards in rows on 2 needles

1st row – Sl 1, Purl to end.

2nd row – *Sl 1, K1, rep from* to last st, K1.

Rep these 2 rows 12 times and then 1st row once.

Turn Heel

Knit 17, Sl 1, K1, psso, K1, turn, P6, P2tog, P1, turn, K7, Sl 1, K1, psso, K1, turn, P8, P2tog, P1, K9, Sl 1, K1, psso, K1, turn, cont in this manner until all sts are worked on to one needle…18 sts. Knit back first 9 sts. Heel is now complete. Slip all instep sts back on to one needle.

Shape Foot

Change back to variegated yarn.

First needle – Knit 9 heel sts, pick up and knit 16 sts along first side of heel; Second needle – knit across instep sts; Third needle – pick up and knit 16 sts along other side of heel knit rem 9 heel sts. Knitting is now back in the round.

Decrease for instep

1st round – Knit.

2nd round – First needle – Knit to last 4 sts, K2tog, K2; Second needle – Knit; Third needle – K2, Sl 1, K1, psso, Knit to end.

Rep these two rounds until 15 sts rem on needle one and three and 30 sts rem on needle two. Cont in stocking st without further shaping until work measures 15cm (6in) from where sts were picked up at side of heel.

Toe Shaping

Change back to pale pink yarn.

1st round – Knit.

2nd round – First needle – Knit to last 4sts, K2tog, K2; Second needle – K2, K1, Sl 1, psso K to last 4 sts K2tog, K2; Third needle – K2, Sl 1, K1, psso, Knit to end.

Rep these 2 rounds until 7 sts rem on needle one and three and 14 sts rem on needle two. Slip sts from third needle on to end of first needle thus completing the round.

Toe is now ready for grafting (refer to page 12 for instructions).Darn in any loose ends. Press lightly if needed.

"OVER THE RAINBOW" STRIPED SOCKS

These little socks were lucky to make it into the book as both Elsie and Fin, my grandchildren, were very keen to nab them as they came hot off the needles! I had to reassure them that they would be knitted their own pair of "Rainbow" socks just as soon as I finished all the other socks. The leg and foot length can both be lengthened in these socks but just make sure you have enough yarn if you are making them using leftover bits of 4 ply.

SKILL LEVEL
Intermediate knitting skills

SIZE
Child's foot (UK 8.5, EUR 25.5, US 9.5)
Foot length – 16cm (6½in) (length can be altered)

TENSION
38 sts and 48 rows to 10cm (4in) of stocking st worked on 2.25mm (UK 13, US 1) double pointed knitting needles.
Be sure to measure tension carefully. If less sts try using one size smaller needles. If more sts try using one size larger needles.

MATERIALS
Yarn:
- 25 g (1 oz) of 3 shades 4 ply. I have used dark purple, bright pink and aqua for the cuffs and feet.
- Small amounts, (less than 25 g (1 oz)) of 7 other 4 ply shades for the stripes.

Knitting Needles:
- 1 set of 4, 2.25mm (UK 13, US 1) double pointed knitting needles.
- Wool needle for darning in ends and grafting toe.

Socks
(Make 2)
Using a set of 4, 2.25mm (UK 13, US 1) double pointed knitting needles, cast on 54 sts…18,18,18.

Work in K1, P1 Rib for 7.5cm (3in).

Change to stocking st and work in stripe pattern of 2 rounds for each stripe. Decide on stripe pattern and work 2 complete sets of stripes plus 2 more rounds, a total of 36 rounds.

Commence Heel

K15 st from first needle, turn, P15, P15, from third needle, (these 30 sts are for the heel).

Divide rem sts between 2 needles and leave for instep. Decide which color you want to use for heel. Heel is worked backwards and forwards on 2 needles.

1st row – Sl 1, Knit to end.

2nd row – Sl1, purl to end.

Rep these 2 rows a further 8 times.

Turn Heel

Next row – K17, Sl 1, K1, psso, K1, turn, P6, P2tog, P1, turn, K7, Sl !, K1, psso, K1, turn, P8, P2tog, P1, turn, K9, Sl 1, K1, psso, K1, turn. Cont in this manner until all sts have been worked onto one needle and 18 sts rem. Knit back 9 sts.

Choose another color for foot

Slip all instep sts back on to one needle…24 sts.

Taking desired color for foot and starting at centre back of heel with new needle knit 9 sts of heel and then pick up and knit 10 sts along side of heel. With second needle knit across instep sts. With third needle pick up and knit 10 sts along other side of heel knit rem 9 heel sts. Knit one round.

Shape Instep

1st round – First needle – Knit to last 3 sts, K2tog, K1; Second needle – Knit; Third needle – K1, Sl 1, K1, psso, Knit to end.

2nd round – Knit.

Rep these 2 rounds until 12 sts rem on needle one and three and 24 sts rem on needle two. Work a further 32 rounds without shaping.

Shape toe

Decide which color you would like to use for the toe and change to this color.

1st round – First needle – Knit to last 3 sts, K2tog, K1; Second needle – K1, Sl 1, K1, psso, knit to last 3 sts, K2tog, K1; Third needle – K1, Sl 1, K1, psso. Knit to end.

2nd round – Knit.

Rep these 2 rounds until 5 sts rem on needle one and three and 10 sts rem on needle two. Knit one round and then first needle of next round. Slip sts from third needle on to end of first needle thus completing the round.

Toe is now ready for grafting (refer to page 12 for instructions). Darn in all ends. Press lightly if needed.

Make another sock to match, using a different contrast for the top ribbing and the toe.

DELFT

These lovely ankle length ladies' socks are a good introduction to Fair Isle knitting in the round. Featuring a straightforward two color graph they nevertheless achieve a great result. The traditional ribbed sock top is hidden under the color work.

Always remember to turn your sock inside out just prior to commencing your heel section or your sock will not have its color panel sitting neatly on the outside.

SKILL LEVEL
Intermediate knitting skills

SIZE
Ladies small to medium foot (UK 5–8, EUR 37–42, US 7.5–10.5)
Cuff section measures 6cm (2½ in)

TENSION
38 sts and 48 rows to 10cm (4in) of stocking st worked on 2.25mm (UK 13, US 1) double pointed knitting needles.
Be sure to measure tension carefully. If less sts try using one size smaller needles. If more sts try using one size larger needles.

MATERIALS
Yarn:
- 1 x 100 g (3½ oz) ball of 4 ply, Heritage Sock Wool in Delft Blue.
- 1 x 50 g (2 oz) ball of 4 ply, Cream Sock Wool.

Knitting Needles:
- 1 set of 4, 2.25mm (UK 13, US 1) double pointed knitting needles.
- Wool needle for grafting toe and darning in ends.

Socks
(Make 2)
Using a set of 4, 2.25mm (UK 13, US 1) double pointed knitting needles and 4 ply Delft Blue, cast on 72 sts…24,24,24. Join into a ring being careful not to twist the stitches.
Work 5 rounds of K1, P1 rib.
Continue in stocking stitch working from the chart (see page 52) from right to left until all 25 rounds have been worked.
Work a further 26 rounds K1, P1 rib.

Decrease Round – * K1, P1, 8 times K2tog, rep from * to end of round…68 sts.

Heel – Slip 10 sts from end of second needle on to the beginning of the third needle, these 32 sts are for the heels.

Turn the knitting inside out.

Divide the rem sts between two needles and leave for the instep.

1st row – *Sl 1, K1, rep from * to last st, K1.

2nd row – Sl 1, Purl to end.

Rep these two rows a further 14 times

Turn heel – K19, Sl 1, K1, psso, K1, turn, P8, P2tog, P1, turn, K9, Sl 1, K1, psso, K1, turn, P10, P2tog, P1, turn, K11, Sl 1, K1, psso, K1, turn, cont in this manner until all sts are worked onto one needle and 20 sts rem. Knit back 10 sts. Heel is now complete. Slip all instep sts back on to one needle. Take one needle and knit 10 heel sts, pick up and knit 17 sts along side of heel. With another needle knit across instep sts. With another needle pick up and knit 17 sts along other side of heel, knit rem 10 heel sts. Knitting is now back in the round. Work one round dec 2 sts evenly on needle 2.

Shape instep

1st round – Knit.

2nd round – First needle – Knit to last 4 sts, K2tog, K2; Second needle – Knit; Third needle – K2, Sl 1, K1 psso, knit to end.

Rep these two rounds until 17 sts rem on needle one and three and 34 sts rem on needle two.

Knit one round.

Work the first 6 rounds of the chart again.

Continue without further shaping until foot measures 15cm (6in) from where sts were picked up at side of heel (or length desired).

Work first 6 rounds of graph again.

Shape Toe

1st round – Knit.

2nd round – First needle -– Knit to last 4 sts, K2tog, K2; Second needle – K2, Sl 1, K1, psso, knit to last 4 sts, K2tog, K2; Third needle – K2, Sl 1, K1 psso, Knit to end.

Rep these 2 rounds until 8 sts rem on needle one and three and 16 sts rem on needle two. Knit one round and then first needle of next round. Slip sts from third needle on to end of first needle thus completing the round.

Toe is now ready for grafting (refer to page 12 for instructions).

Make another sock to match, using a different contrast for the top ribbing and the toe.

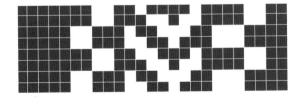

RUBY LACE SOCKS

These lace patterned socks are a great pair to make if you would like to embark on lace knitting in the round for the first time. The pattern is a four row repeat which is easy to remember and the leg and foot length can be lengthened as desired. Just bear in mind that you will require extra yarn if you want to make them much longer.

SKILL LEVEL
Intermediate knitting skills

SIZE
Ladies small to medium foot (UK 6–8, EUR 39–42, US 8.5–10.5)
Leg length – 10cm (4in) to heel

TENSION
38 sts and 46 rows to 10cm (4in) of stocking st worked on 2.75mm (12 UK, 2 US) double pointed knitting needles.
Measure tension carefully. If fewer sts try using one size smaller needles. If more sts, try using one size larger needles.

MATERIALS
Yarn:
- 1 x 100 g (3½ oz) ball of 4 ply, Hedgehog Fibres Sock Yarn (Shade used was Merlot). Alternate 4 ply sock yarns will be suitable.

Knitting Needles:
- 1 set of 4, 2.25mm (UK 13, US 1) double pointed knitting needles.
- 1 set of 4, 2.75mm (12 UK, 2 US) double pointed knitting needles.
- Wool needle for grafting toe and darning in ends.

Socks
(Make 2)
Using a set of 4, 2.25mm (UK 13, US 1) double pointed knitting needles and 4 ply Hedgehog Fibres, cast on 64 sts …22,20,22.
Join into a ring, careful not to twist the sts.
Work in K1, P1 rib for 3cm (1¼in).
Change to 2.75mm (12 UK, 2 US) double pointed knitting needles and begin lace pattern.
1st round – * P2, YO, K2tog, P2, Knit 2nd stitch on left hand needle, then first

stitch on left hand needle and slip both stitches off together (twist), repeat from * to end of round.

2nd round – P2, K2, repeat from * to end of round.

3rd round – *P2, K2tog, yen, P2, Knit 2nd stitch on left hand needle, then first stitch on left hand needle and slip both stitches off together (twist), rep from * to end of round.

4th round – As for 2nd round.

Repeat these 4 rounds until work measures 10cm (4in) from cast on edge, ending with a 4th pattern round.

Next round – First needle – Work in pattern for 1st 17 sts for heel; Second and Third needles, slip 32 sts on to 2 needles for instep. Slip rem 15 sts on to end of 1st needle for heel.

Note – Heel is worked backwards and forwards in rows.

1st row – Sl 1, Purl to end.

2nd row – *Sl 1, K1, rep from * to last st, K1.

Rep these 2 rows 12 times and then 1st row once.

Shape Heel

Next row – K23, Sl 1, K1, paso, turn, P15, P2tog, turn, K15, Sl1, K1, psso, turn, P15, P2tog, turn, K15, Sl 1, K1, psso, turn, cont in this manner until all sts are worked on to one needle and 16 sts rem, ending with a purl row. Turn and knit back 8 sts. Place all instep sts back on to one needle and proceed as follows.

Shape Instep

Starting at centre heel – K8, pick up and knit 16 sts down first side of heel. With next needle Patt across instep sts, with next needle pick up and knit 16 sts along other side of heel, knit rem 8 heel sts. Knitting is now back in the round.

1st round – First needle – Knit to last 4 sts, K2tog, K2; Second needle – Patt across instep sts; Third needle – K2, Sl 1, K1, psso, knit to end.

2nd round – Knit on needle one and three and keep patt correct on needle 2.

Rep these two rounds until 16 sts rem on needle one and three and 32 sts rem on needle two.

Cont in patt without further shaping until work measures 15cm (6in) from where sts were picked up at side of heel.

Shape Toe

1st round – First needle – Knit to last 4 sts, K2tog, K2; Second needle – K2, Sl 1, K1, psso, knit to last 4 sts, K2tog, K2; Third needle – K2, Sl 1, K1, psso, knit to end.

2nd round – Knit.

Rep these two rounds until 7 sts rem on needle one and three and 14 sts rem on needle two. Knit one more round, finishing by knitting all the stitches from needle one on to needle three.

Toe is now ready for grafting (refer to page 12 for instructions).

FRENCH NAVY

These ladies' calf length striped socks are a great project for the sock knitter who has developed a little bit of confidence with their knitting and is ready to try something more than just the basic plain sock. These socks have some shaping down the back of the leg so they will stay in place nicely and fit the shape of your leg well as they taper towards the ankle. Blue and white stripes give a lovely fresh appeal but you can choose any colors which appeal. It is possible to make the leg and foot longer, but you will need extra yarn.

SKILL LEVEL
Intermediate knitting skills

SIZE
Ladies small to medium foot – (UK 5–8, EUR 38–42, US 7.5–10.5)
Leg length – 24cm (9½in) to heel shaping (leg length can be lengthened)

TENSION
38 sts and 44 rows to 10cm (4in) of stocking st using 2.25mm (UK 13, US 1) double pointed knitting needles.

Please measure tension carefully. If fewer sts try using one size smaller needles. If more sts, try using one size larger needles.

MATERIALS
Yarn:
- 1 x 100 g (3½ oz) hank of 4 ply Rowan Fine Art (Merino wool, Kid Mohair and Mulberry Silk) shade used – 313.
- 1 x 50 g (2 oz) ball of Patons Patonyle 4 ply Sock Wool 75% Wool, 25% Nylon.

Knitting Needles:
- 1 set of 4, 2.25mm (UK 13, US 1) double pointed knitting needles.
- Wool needle for grafting toe.

Socks
(Make 2)
Using a set of 4, 2.25mm (UK 13, US 1) double pointed knitting needles and 4 ply Rowan Fine Art, cast on 68 sts… 22,24,22. Join into a ring being careful not to twist the sts.
Work in rounds of K1, P1, Rib for 6cm (2½ in).
Change to Stripe Pattern
Stripe pattern is as follows – 4 rounds Rowan Fine Art, 4 rounds Cream.

Work a total of 10 stripes.

Commence Shaping for Calf

Next round – K1, Sl 1, paso, Knit to last 3 sts, K2tog, K1 – at same time keep stripe pattern correct. Knit a further 5 round st st in stripe pattern.

Repeat the last 6 rounds until 62 sts rem.

Cont in stripe pattern without further shaping until leg measures 24cm (9½ in) from cast on edge.

Divide for Heel

Note – heel is worked backwards and forward in rows on 2 needles using Rowan Fine Art only and the remainder of the sts which are for the instep are held on the rem 2 needles.

Next – Knit the first 15 sts, slip the last 15 sts from needle three onto the same needle (these are the heel sts). Divide the remaining sts between 2 needles and leave for instep.

1st row – Sl 1, Purl to end.

2nd row – *Sl 1, K1, rep from* to last st, K1.

Rep these 2 rows 12 times and then 1st row once.

Turn Heel – Knit 20, turn, P10, turn, K9, Sl 1, K1, psso, K1, turn, P10, P2tog, P1, turn, K11, Sl 1, K1, psso, K1, turn, P12, P2tog, P1, turn, K13, Sl1, K1, psso, K1, turn P14, P2tog, P1, cont in this manner until all sts are worked onto one needle…18 sts.

Knit back 8 sts.

Place all instep sts back on to one needle.

Shape Instep and Foot

K10, pick up and knit 16 sts down side of heel. With next needle knit across instep sts. With next needle pick up and knit 16 sts along other side of heel, knit rem 8 sts.

Knitting is now back in the round.

1st round – Knit

2nd round – First needle – Knit to last 4 sts, K2tog, K2; Second needle – Knit; Third needle – K2, Sl 1, K1, psso. Knit to end.

Rep these 2 rounds until 16 sts rem on needle one and three and 32 sts on needle two.

Cont without further shaping until foot measures 15cm (6in) from where sts were picked up from side of heel.

Shape Toe – (change to Cream Patonyle)

1st round – Knit.

2nd round – 1st needle – Knit to last 4 sts, K2tog, K2; 2nd needle – K2, Sl 1, K1, psso, Kto last 4sts, K2tog, K2; 3rd needle – K2, Sl 1, K1, psso. Knit to end.

Rep these 2 rounds until 7 sts rem on needle one and three and 14 sts on needle two. Knit one more round, finishing by knitting all the stitches from needle one on to needle three.

Toe is now ready for grafting (refer to page 12 for instructions).

KNEE HIGH BLUE BOOT SOCKS

These lovely thick 8 ply socks will be great for gardening in Winter or for wearing with boots. If you are new to knitting socks, 8 ply can be a bit easier to get started with as the tension is easier to maintain and the stripe pattern allows you to see where you have got to with your decreases. If you are not keen on stripes you can knit them plain, just bear in mind you will need 3 x 50 g (2 oz) balls of the same colored yarn.

SKILL LEVEL
Intermediate knitting skills

SIZE
Ladies small to medium foot (UK 5–8, EUR 38–42, US 7.5–10.5)

TENSION
25 sts and 34 rows to 10cm (4in) in width measured over stocking st using 3.25mm (UK 10, US 3) double pointed knitting needles. Check your tension. If less sts try using one size smaller needles. If more sts try using one size larger needles.

MATERIALS
Yarn:
- 1 x 50 g (2 oz) ball of navy blue 8 ply Pure wool (Main Color).
- 1 x 50 g (2 oz) ball of mid blue 8 ply Pure wool (A).
- 1 x 50 g (2 oz) ball of light blue 8 ply Pure wool (B).

Knitting Needles:
- 1 set of 4, 3.25mm (UK 10, US 3) double pointed knitting needles.
- Wool needle for grafting toe and darning in ends.

Stripe Pattern - Stocking Stitch (every round knit)
2 rounds Main Color
2 rounds A
2 rounds B

Socks
(Make 2)
Using a set of 4, 3.25mm (UK 10, US 3) double pointed knitting needles and main color 8 ply (navy blue), cast on 64 sts …22,20,22.

Join into a ring being careful not to twist the stitches.

1st round – *K1tbl, P1, rep from* to end of round.

Rep this round until work measures 7.5cm (3in) from cast on edge.

Slip last st off first needle on to beg of second needle and first st of third needle on to end of second needle, 21,22,21 sts.

Commence Stripe pattern

Work in Stripe pattern until work measures 15cm (6in) from cast on edge.

Calf Shaping

Next round – (Keep continuity of Stripe Patt correct) – K1, K2tog, knit to last 3 sts, K1, Sl 1, psso.

Work 5 rounds Stripe patt.

Repeat these 6 rounds a further 3 times, 56 sts.

Continue in Stripe patt without further shaping until leg measures 30cm (12in) from cast on edge.

Begin Heel

Note – Heel is worked backwards and forwards in rows on 2 needles in a solid color (light blue) and the remainder of the stitches are held on 2 needles for the instep.

Next row – Knit the first 14 sts of round on to a needle, slip the last 14 sts of the round (needle 3) on to the same needle, 28 heel sts. Divide the rem sts between two needles and leave for the instep.

Using Shade B

1st row – Sl1, Purl to end.

2nd row – *Sl 1, K1, rep from * to last st, K1.

Repeat these 2 rows a further 9 times and then first row once…21 heel rows.

Turn Heel – K17, K1, Sl 1, psso, K1, turn. P8, P2tog, P1, turn, K9, Sl 1, K1, psso, K1, turn, P10, P2tog, P1, turn, cont in this manner until all sts are worked on to one needle…18 sts.

Knit back the first 9 sts (this completes the heel). Slip all the instep sts back on to one needle.

Note – Foot will be worked in Mid Blue and Toe in Main Color

Using another needle, knit rem 9 heel sts and then pick up and knit 13 sts along side of heel; with a second needle knit across instep sts; using a third needle pick up and knit 13 sts along other side of heel, knit rem 9 heel sts. Knitting is now back in the round.

Shape Instep

1st round – Knit.

2nd round – First needle – Knit to last 4sts, K2tog, K2; Second needle – Knit; Third needle – K2, Sl 1, K1, psso. Knit to end.

Repeat these two rounds until 14 sts rem on needle one and three and 28 sts rem on needle two.

Cont without further shaping until foot measures 14(15,16)cm (5½(6,6½)in) from where sts were picked up at side of heel.

Shape Toe – Change color for toe

1st round – Knit.

2nd round – First needle – Knit to last 4sts, K2tog, K2; Second needle – K2, Sl 1, K1, psso, K to last 4sts, K2tog, K2; Third needle – K2, Sl 1, K1, psso. Knit to end.

Repeat these 2 rounds until 20 sts rem, 5 sts on needle one and three and 10 sts on needle two.

Knit one round and then first needle of next round. Slip sts from third needle on to end of first needle thus completing the round.

Toe is now ready for grafting (refer to page 12 for instructions).

LITTLE BOXES

This is a great pair of socks for the new sock knitter who is keen to have a try at a pattern but is a bit daunted by 4 ply. The 8 ply checkerboard pattern gives a lovely textured result and the addition of the ruby stripes gives these socks a very sprightly look. By adjusting the foot length they are suitable for ladies or men. Just be aware that if you are going to make them significantly longer you may need an extra ball of yarn so buy that at the time so you can be sure of your dye lots.

SKILL LEVEL
Intermediate knitting skills

SIZE
Ladies medium foot (UK 6–8, EUR 39–42, US 8.5–10.5)
Leg length – 22cm (8½in) from heel to toe (can be varied)

TENSION
28 sts to 10cm (4 in) in width measured over checkerboard pattern on 3.25mm (UK 10, US 3) double pointed knitting needles.

MATERIALS
Yarn:
- 3 x 50 g (2 oz) balls of 8 ply Dark Grey Merino (DK).
- 1 x 50 g (2 oz) ball of 8 ply Ruby Merino (DK).

Note – buy extra if length is increased

Knitting Needle:
- 1 set of 4, 3.25mm (UK 10, US 3) double pointed knitting needles.
- Wool needle for grafting toe and darning in ends.

Socks
(Make 2)
Using the set of double pointed knitting needles and Dark Grey Merino, cast on 56 sts …18,20,18. Join into a ring being careful not to twist sts.

Work in K2, P2 Rib for 10 rounds dark grey. 2 rounds Ruby, 2 rounds Dark Grey, 2 round Ruby, 10 rounds Dark Grey.

Commence checkerboard pattern. The pattern is * K4, P4. Repeat for 4 rows and then reversed *P4, K4. See Chart (p. 66).

Work in pattern for 10cm (4in). You should have 9 little boxes if your tension is correct.

Commence Heel

Slip last 10 sts from third needle on to the end of first needle, 28 sts. Divide rem sts between two needles and leave for instep.

Note – Heel is worked backwards and forwards in rows.

1st row – Sl 1, Purl to end.

2nd row – *Sl 1, K1, rep from* to last st, K1.

Rep these two rows a further 11 times and then first row once.

Turn Heel – K18, Sl 1, K1, psso, K1, turn, P8, P2tog, P1, turn, K7, Sl 1, K1, psso, K1, turn, P8, P2tog, P1, turn, K9, Sl 1, K1, psso, K1, turn, cont in this manner until all sts are worked on to one needle, 18 sts, knit back 9 sts. Heel is now complete. Slip all instep sts back on to one needle.

Foot Shaping

Knit 9 heel sts, pick up and knit 14 sts along first side of heel. On another needle knit across instep sts. With another needle pick up and knit 14 sts along other side of heel. Knitting is now back in the round.

1st round – Knit.

2nd round – First needle – Knit to last 4 sts, K2tog, K2; Second needle – Pattern (keeping checkerboard pattern correct); Third needle – K2, Sl 1, K1, psso. Knit to end.

Rep these 2 rounds until 14 sts rem on needle one and three and 28 sts on needle two.

Cont without further shaping until foot measures 14cm (5½in) from where sts were picked up from side of heel.

Change to Ruby 8 ply for Toe Shaping

1st round – Knit.

2nd round – First needle – Knit to last 4 sts, K2tog, K2; Second needle – K2, Sl 1, K1, psso, Kto last 4 sts, K2tog, K2; Third needle – K2, Sl 1, K1, psso. Knit to end.

Rep these 2 rounds until 7 sts rem on needle one and three and 14 sts on needle two. Knit one more round, finishing by knitting all the stitches from needle one on to needle three.

Toe is now ready for grafting (refer to page 12 for instructions). Darn in any loose ends.

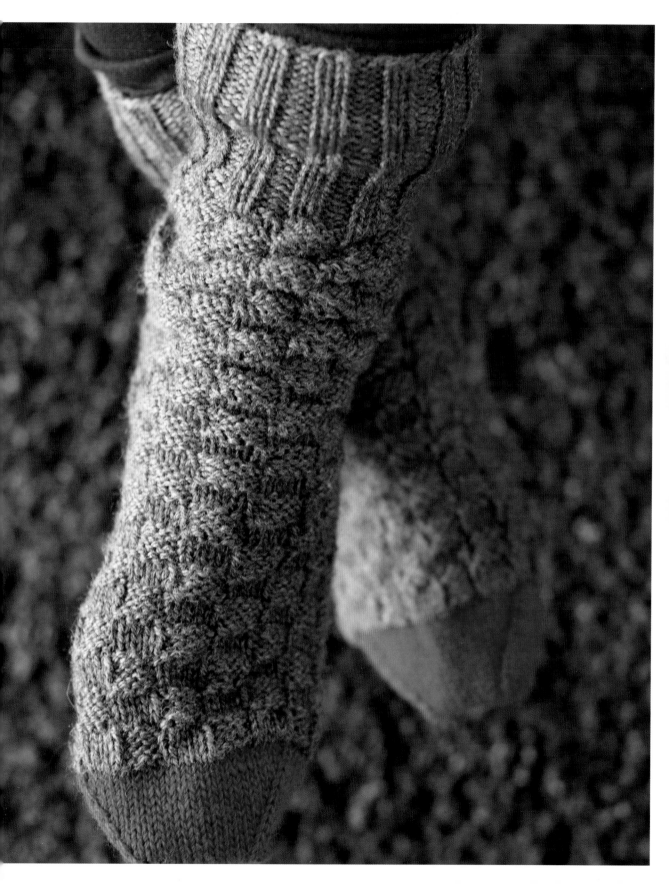

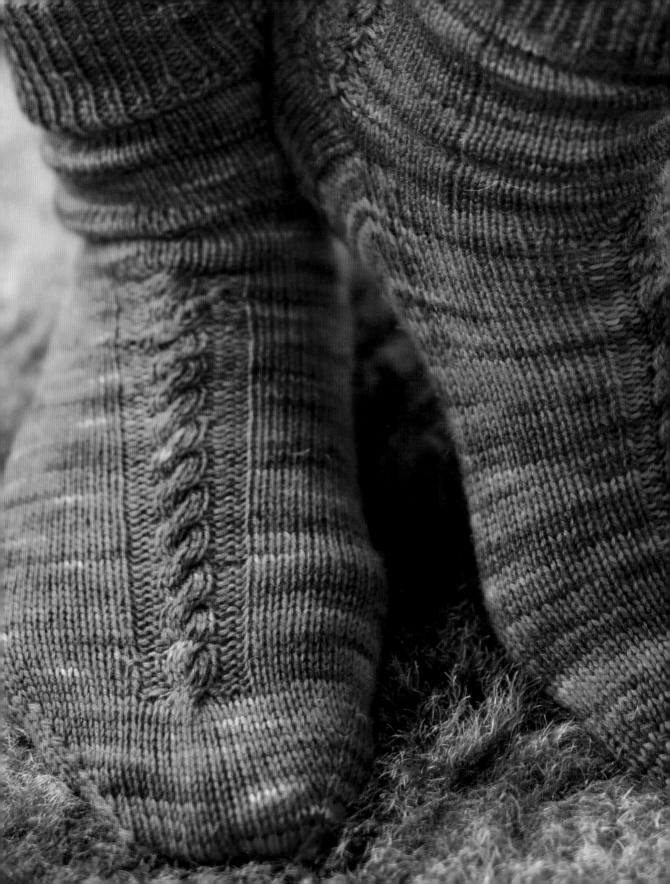

RED CABLE SOCKS

These lovely socks have and elegant cable down each side and then the same one repeated on the front of the foot. The use of a beautiful variegated sock yarn will set the cable off well.

SKILL LEVEL
Intermediate knitting skills

SIZE
Ladies small to medium foot (UK 4–5.5, EUR 37–38.5, US 6–8)
Leg length – 12cm (4½in) to heel

TENSION
36 sts and 44 rows to 10cm (4in) worked over stocking st on 2.25mm (UK 13, US 1) double pointed knitting needles.

If your tension is loose – i.e. too few stitches per 10cm (4in), try using one size smaller needles i.e. 2.00mm (UK 14, US 0). If your tension is tight – i.e. too many stitches, try using one size larger needles i.e. 2.75mm (UK 12, US 2).

MATERIALS
Yarn:
- 2 x 50 g (2 oz) balls of Merino/ Possum, 70/30 sock wool. Hand Dyed. The yarn comes in hanks and you will need to wind it into balls before knitting. (Available online) Note – any other 4 ply sock yarn would be equally successful.

Knitting Needles:
- 1 set of 4, 2.25mm (UK 13, US 1) double pointed knitting needles or size required for correct tension.
- Wool needle for grafting toe.
- Fine Cable Needle

SPECIAL ABBREVIATION
C6R – Slip next 3 stitches onto cable needle and hold at back of work, knit 3 and then knit 3 from cable needle.

Cable Pattern
This is a five row repeat
1st row – P2, C6R, P2.
2nd row – P2, K6, P2.
3rd row – P2, K6, P2.
4th row – P2, K6, P2.
5th row – P2, K6, P2.

Socks
(Make 2)

Using a set of 4, 2.25mm (UK 13, US 1) double pointed knitting needles and merino/possum sock yarn, cast on 72 sts… 24,24,24. Join into a round being careful not to twist the stitches.

Work 20 rounds of K1, P1 rib.

Next round – Knit, increasing 4 sts evenly on needle one and on needle three, 80 sts.

Next round – Knit.

Begin Cable pattern

1st round – First needle – K9, P2, C6R, P2.K9; Second needle – Knit; Third needle – K9, P2, C6R, P2, K9.

2nd round – First needle – K9, P2, K6, P2, K9; Second needle – Knit; Third needle – K9, P2, K6, P2, K9.

3rd round – First needle – K9, P2, K6, P2, K9; Second needle – Knit; Third needle – K9, P2, K6, P2, K9.

4th round – First needle – K9, P2, K6, P2, K9; Second needle – Knit; Third needle – K9, P2, K6, P2, K9.

5th round – First needle – K9, P2, K6, P2, K9; Second needle – Knit; Third needle – K9,P2, K6, P2, K9.

Repeat these five rounds until 8 cable twists have been completed. Leg length should be approx 11.5cm (4½in).

Next round – Knit, decreasing 4 sts evenly on First and Third needles, 72 sts.

Divide for Heel

Knit first 18 sts on to empty needle, slip last 18 sts from needle three onto this same needle. These will be the heel sts and will be worked backwards and forward is rows.

Place all remaining sts on 2 needles (These will become the instep sts)

1st row – Sl 1, Purl to end.

2nd row – *Sl 1, K1, rep from* ending with K1.

Repeat these 2 rows a further 13 times and 1st row once.

Turn Heel – Knit 23, turn, P10, turn, K9, Sl1, K1, paso, K1, turn, P10, P2tog, P1, turn, K11, Sl1, K1, paso, K1, turn, P12, P2tog, P1, turn, cont in this manner until all stitches have been worked on to one needle.

Place instep stitches back on to one needle.

Picking up stitches along side of heel

Knit half the heel sts on to the empty needle. You will now have your heel sts on two needles and your instep sts on one needle.

Beginning at the centre of the heel, knit the first half of the heel sts and then pick up and knit 17 sts along the right side of the heel. On the next needle, knit across instep sts: on the next needle pick up and knit 17 sts along left side of heel and knit rem heel sts.

Knitting is now back in the round.
Knit one round, dec 2 sts evenly on instep
needle 32 sts.

Foot shaping

1st round – knit to last four sts, K2tog k2;
Second needle – K12,, P2, C6R, P2.K12;
Third needle – K2, Sl1, K1, paso. Knit to
end.

2nd round – First needle – Knit; Second
needle – K12, P2, K6, P2, K12; Third
needle – Knit.

Cont in this manner dec on alt rows until
16 sts rem on needle one and three and
at the same time keeping 5 row cable st
pattern correct as set.

Cont without further shaping but
continuing to keep cable pattern correct
until 16 cable twists have been worked.

Note – Foot can be made longer at this
stage but bear in mind you may need
more yarn. This pair of socks used fairly
close to 100 g (3½ oz).

Shape Toe

Toe is worked in stocking stitch only

1st round – First needle – Knit to last 4
sts, K2tog, K2; Second needle – K2, Sl1,
K1 paso, K to last 4 sts, K2tog, K2; Third
needle – K2, Sl 1, K1, psso, K to end.

2nd round – Knit.

Repeat these 2 rounds until there are 7 sts
rem on needle one and three and 14 sts
on needle two.

Knit one more round, finishing by knitting
all the stitches from needle one on to
needle three.

Toe is now ready for grafting (refer to page
12 for instructions).

SUPER SOFT SLIPPER SOCKS

There comes a time in every knitter's life when they want to make socks. Socks are great. They involve no sewing up. a great bonus, and can be easily tailored to fit different sized feet. This is a great beginners sock project as they are knitted in 8 ply and have relatively little shaping. Take your time and remember that with the exception of the heel you will be knitting round and round so every round is a knit, (no purl rounds). These slipper socks have a rolled cuff and a ribbed panel around the ankle to hold them snuggly in place.

SKILL LEVEL
Intermediate knitting skills

SIZE
Ladies small to medium foot (UK 5–8, EUR 38–42, US 7.5–10.5)
Length can be adjusted

TENSION
26 sts and 26 rows to 10cm (4in) measured over stocking st on 3.75mm (UK 9, US 5) double pointed knitting needles.
Note – This tension is tighter than would normally be used for 8 ply, but you want a fairly firm fabric for socks.

MATERIALS
Yarn:
- 2 x 50 g (2 oz) balls of 8 ply, Main Color pure wool.
- 1 x 50 g (2 oz) ball of 8 ply, Contrast Color pure wool

Knitting Needles:
- 1 set of 4, 3.75mm (UK 9, US 5) double pointed knitting needles.
- Wool needle for grafting toe.

Slipper Socks
(Make 2)
Using a set of 4, 3.75mm (UK 9, US 5) double pointed knitting needles, and 8 ply yarn in Contrast Color, cast on 42 sts… 22,10,10.

Cuff
Work 10 rounds st st (every round knit)
Work a further 5 rounds K1, P1 rib. Break off Contrast Color and join in Main Color.

Heel

The heel will now be worked backwards and forward in rows on the first 22 sts in main color.

With right side facing proceed as follows.

1st row – Sl 1, *K1, Sl 1, K1 rep from * to end of row.

2nd row – S1, Purl to end of row.

Rep these 2 rows a further 12 times, 26 rows in total.

To Turn Heel

With right side facing you proceed as follows

1st row – Sl 1, K12, Sl 1, K1, psso, K1, turn.

2nd row – SL 1, P5, P2tog, P1, turn

3rd row – Sl 1, K6, Sl 1, K1, psso, K1, turn.

4th row – SL 1, P7, P2tog, P1, turn.

5th row – Sl 1, K8, Sl 1, K1, psso, K1, turn.

6th row – SL 1, P9, P2tog, P1, turn.

7th row – Sl 1, K10, Sl 1, K1, psso, K1, turn.

8th row – SL 1, P11, P2tog, P1, turn.

14 Heel stitches now remain.

To complete your heel you now need to pick up your heel gusset stitches. These are stitches down the straight side of the heel. To do this proceed as follows.

First – Slip all the instep stitches (these are the stitches held on the remaining two needles on to one needle).

Next – With right side of the work facing you, knit the first 7 of the heels stitches. Take a new needle and knit the next 7 remaining heel stitches. With this same needle pick up and knit 14 stitches along the edge of the heel flap. With another needle, knit across the 20 instep stitches. With a new needle, pick up and knit 14 stitches along other side of heel flap, with this same needle knit remaining 7 heel stitches, 62 stitches in total. 42 sole stitches and 20 instep stitches.

Shaping the Instep

1st round – Knit all stitches.

2nd round – First needle – Knit to last 4 stitches K2tog, K2; Second needle – Knit; Third needle – Knit 2, Slip 1, Knit 1 psso, knit remaining stitches.

Repeat these two rounds until 11 sts remain on needle one and three and 20 sts remain on needle two, 42 sts.

Continue knitting without further shaping until foot measures 15cm (6in) from where stiches were picked up at side of heel (this will give a UK size 6–7 slipper). You can increase the length of your slipper at this point if you desire.

Shape Toe

Break off Main Color and join in contrast. Knit one round.

1st round – Knit.

2nd round – First needle – Knit to last 4 sts, K2tog, K2; Second needle – Knit; Third needle – K2, Sl 1, K1, psso, Knit to end.

3rd round – First needle – Knit to last 4 sts, K2tog, K2; Second needle – K2, Sl 1, K1, psso, knit to last 4 sts, K2tog , K2; Third

needle – K2, Sl 1, K1, psso, Knit to end.
Repeat rounds 1 and 3 until 5 sts remain
on needle one and three and 10 sts
remain on needle two.

Toe is now ready for grafting (refer to page
12 for instructions). Darn in all loose ends
and press lightly if needed.

Graft Toe
Slip stitches from needle three onto
needle one so that you have 2 lots of 10
sts facing each other.

TURKISH DELIGHT

The color of these socks reminds me of the inside of the Turkish Delight sweet. They will certainly keep your feet warm as they are knitted with a mix of alpaca and possum yarn making them both soft and hard wearing. If pink is not to your taste just pick another color. The narrow stripes mean that you can successfully carry the yarn without having to break the yarn off after every stripe.

SKILL LEVEL
Intermediate knitting skills

SIZE
Ladies small to medium foot (UK 5–8, EUR 38–42, US 7.5–10.5)
Leg Length – 24cm (9½in) to heel

TENSION
35sts and 40 rows to 10cm (4in) in width over stocking st worked on 2.25mm (UK 13, US 1) double pointed knitting needles.

Measure tension carefully. If less sts try using one size smaller needles. If more sts try using one size larger needles.

MATERIALS
Yarn:
- 1 x 50 g (2 oz) ball of 4 ply, Possum/Alpaca/Merino sock yarn, Plum.
- 1 x 50 g (2 oz) ball of 4 ply, Possum/Alpaca/Merino sock yarn, Bright Pink.

Knitting Needle:
- 1 set of 4, 2.25mm (UK 13, US 1) double pointed knitting needles.
- Wool needle for grafting toe and darning in ends.

Socks
(Make 2)
Using a set of 4, 2.25mm (UK 13, US 1) double pointed knitting needles and Plum 4 ply, cast on 66 sts, 22,22,22. Join in to a ring being careful not to twist sts.
Work in K2, P2 rib for 8cm (3in).

Commence Stripe Pattern
Work in Stripes of 2 rounds Plum, 2 rounds Bright Pink.
Work a total of 28 stripes for leg.
Divide for Heel
Note – Heel is worked backwards and forward in rows on 2 needles using Bright

Pink and the remainder of the sts which are for the instep are held on the rem 2 needles.

Next – Knit the first 15 sts, slip the last 15 sts from needle three onto the same needle (these are the heel sts) divide the remaining sts between 2 needles and leave for instep.

1st row – Sl 1, Purl to end.

2nd row – *Sl 1, K1, rep from* to last st, K1.

Rep these 2 rows 12 times and then 1st row once.

Turn Heel

Knit 20, turn, P10, turn, K9, Sl 1, K1, psso, K1, turn, P10, P2tog, P1, turn, K11, Sl 1, K1, psso, K1, turn, P12, P2tog, P1, turn, K13, Sl1, K1, psso, K1, turn P14, P2tog, P1, cont in this manner until all sts are worked onto one needle, 18 sts.

Knit back 8 sts.

Place all instep sts back on to one needle.

Shape Instep and Foot

Foot is worked In plum only.

K10, pick up and knit 16 sts down side of heel. With next needle knit across instep sts. Next needle pick up and knit 16 sts along other side of heel, knit rem 8 sts.

Knitting is now back in the round.

1st round – Knit (decreasing 2 sts evenly on needle 2).

2nd round – First needle – Knit to last 4 sts, K2tog, K2; Second needle – Knit; Third needle, K2, Sl 1, K1, psso, Knit to end.

Rep these 2 rounds until 16 sts rem on needle one and three and 32 sts on needle two.

Cont without further shaping until foot measures 15cm (6in) from where sts were picked up from side of heel.

Shape Toe

1st round – Knit.

2nd round – First needle – Knit to last 4 sts, K2tog, K2; Second needle – K2, Sl 1, K1, psso, Kto last 4sts, K2tog, K2; Third needle – K2, Sl 1, K1, psso , Knit to end.

Rep these 2 rounds until 7 sts rem on needle one and three and 14 sts on needle two. Knit one more round, finishing by knitting all the stitches from needle one on to needle three.

Toe is now ready for grafting (refer to page 12 for instructions). Darn in all ends and press lightly if required.

KALEIDOSCOPE SOCKS

These socks are a great project for the confident knitter. The circle shapes are knitted first and then assembled in four rounds of five circles to comprise the leg section. The ribbed band is then picked up along the top edge and the heel and foot picked up and knitted from the lower edge. I have knitted these socks in a mixture of merino/possum and alpaca. I love the way the circle shapes are all slightly different, reminding me of looking down a kaleidoscope as a child. You could make your circles in all different colors but by using a variegated yarn.

SKILL LEVEL
Advanced knitting skills

SIZE
Ladies small to medium foot (UK 6–8, EUR 39–42, US 8.5–10.5)
Leg length – 21cm (8¼in) to ankle

TENSION
36 st and 44 rows to 10cm (4in) of st st worked on 2.25mm (UK 13, US 1) double pointed knitting needles using Naturally Waikiwi Yarn.

If your tension is loose try using one size smaller needles. If your tension is too tight, try using one size larger needles.

MATERIALS
Yarn:
- 1 x 50 g (2 oz) ball of Cherry Tree Hill Possum Lace 70% Merino, 30% Possum – Color – Quarry Hill – 450 yards = 50 g (2 oz)
- 2 x 50 g (2 oz) balls of Naturally Waikiwi 55% Merino, 20% Nylon, 15% Alpaca, 10% Possum – Color – Plum – 406 – 198 yards = 50 g (2 oz)
- Both these yarns are 4 ply. Alternate 4 ply sock yarns can be substituted.

Knitting Needles:
- 1 set of 4, 2.25mm (UK 13, US 1) double pointed knitting needles
- Wool needle
- Postal cylinder (this just makes sewing the circles together for the leg much easier, one with approx 23cm (9in) circumference)

Circles

You will need 40 circles for this project. I suggest making them all first. It seems a lot but they are very quick to make and if you end off the centre end of yarn as you go you can use the outer end for joining the circles together.

Using 2.25mm (UK 13, US 1) double pointed knitting needles and Cherry Tree Hill multi colored yarn, cast on 45 sts…15,15,15. Join into a ring being careful not to twist sts.

1st round – Knit.

2nd round – Purl.

3rd round – *K3, K2tog, rep from * to end of round

4th round – Purl.

5th round – *K2, K2tog, rep from * to end of round.

6th round – *Purl.

7th round – *K1, K2tog, rep from * to end of round.

8th round – Purl.

9th round – * K2tog, rep from * all round…6 sts.

10th round – Knit.

11th round – Purl.

12th round – Knit.

Break off yarn, thread through rem sts, pull up tightly and fasten off. Darn in end securely.

Make another 39 circles.

To Make Up

It is easy to do this with the aid of a postal cylinder. Pin the first 5 circles on around the top and stitch them together at the sides for approx 1.5cm (½in). Leave the pins in place.

The second round are pinned in the 'v' shaped gaps below the first row. You will stitch the second row to the top row at two points forming a v shape between two circles of the top row. Do this all the way around, then stitch the second row together at the sides for 1.5cm (½in) the same way you did for the first row. The third row will sit under the second row in the same position as the first row and the fourth row in the same position as the second row. Take your time sewing your circles in place as it will determine the look of your finished sock. Once your four rounds are stitched together you are ready to pick up for the cuff and for the foot. Slide sock off the cylinder.

Sock Top

Using a set of 4, 2.25mm (UK 13, US 1) double pointed knitting needles and Plum 4 ply, pick up and knit 66 sts around the first row of the circles (this becomes the top of the sock). Work 28 rounds of K2, P2 rib. Cast off in rib.

Foot

Using a set of 4, 2.25mm (UK 13, US 1) double pointed knitting needles and Plum 4 ply, pick up and knit 66 sts around the fourth row of circles… 22,22,22.

Work 12 rounds of Stocking stitch (every round knit).

Divide for Heel

Knit first 17 sts of round on to one needle, slip last 17 sts of round on to other end of same needle these 34 sts are for heel. Divide rem sts between two needles and leave for instep.

Note – Heel is worked backwards and forwards in rows on two needles.

1st row – Sl 1, Purl to end.

2nd row – *Sl 1, K1, rep from * to last st.

Rep these 2 rows a further 12 times and then 1st row once.

Turn Heel – Knit 19, Sl 1, K1, psso, K1, turn, P8, P2tog, P1, K7, Sl 1, K1, psso, K1, turn, P8, P2tog, P1, K9, Sl 1, K1, psso, K1, turn, cont in this manner until all sts are worked onto one needle and 20 sts rem. Knit back 10 sts, thus completing heel. Slip all instep sts back on to one needle.

Shape Instep and Foot

K10, pick up and knit 17 sts down side of heel. With next needle knit across instep sts. Next needle pick up and knit 17 sts along other side of heel, knit rem 10 sts.

Knitting is now back in the round.

1st round – Knit.

2nd round – First needle – Knit to last 4 sts, K2tog, K2; Second needle – Knit; Third needle – K2, Sl 1, K1, psso. Knit to end.

Rep these 2 rounds until 17 sts rem on needle one and three and 34 sts on needle two.

Cont without further shaping until foot measures 15cm (6in) from where sts were picked up from side of heel.

Shape Toe

1st round – Knit.

2nd round – First needle – Knit to last 4 sts, K2tog, K2; Second needle – K2, Sl 1, K1, psso, Knit to last 4sts, K2tog, K2; Third needle – K2, Sl 1, K1, psso. Knit to end.

Rep these 2 rounds until 8 sts rem on needle 1 and 3 and 16 sts on needle 3. Knit one more round, finishing by knitting all the stitches from needle one on to needle three.

Toe is now ready for grafting (refer to page 12 for instructions).

PINK FAIR ISLE LADIES ANKLE SOCKS

These traditional style Fair Isle socks are knitted in the round which is great because there is no sewing up. Be careful not to pull the yarn being knitted to tightly otherwise your knitting will not sit flat. If you feel that knitting your Fair Isle section in the round would be really awkward for you it is perfectly fine to knit it on 2 needles and then swap back on to a set of 4 when you come to the rib section.

SKILL LEVEL
Advanced knitting skills

SIZE
Ladies small foot (UK 3, EUR 35.5, US 5)
Foot length – 22cm (8½in)

TENSION
38 sts and 48 rows to 10cm (4in) of stocking st worked on 2.25mm (UK 13, US 1) double pointed knitting needles.

Measure tension carefully. If less sts try using one size smaller needles. If more sts try using one size larger needles.

MATERIALS
Yarn:
- 1 x 100 g (3½ oz) ball of 4 ply, Loopy Legends (Eevi's California Rose) 80% Merino, 20% Nylon.

- 1 x 50 g (2 oz) ball of 4 ply, Dark Pink
- 1 x 50 g (2 oz) ball Dark Purple
- 1 x 50 g (2 oz) ball Variegated Orange
- 1 x 50 g (2 oz) ball, Pale Pink

Knitting Needles:
- 1 Set of 4, 2.25mm (UK 13, US 1) double pointed knitting needles.
- Wool needle for darning in ends and grafting toe.

Socks
(Make 2)
Using a set of 4, 2.25mm (UK 13, US 1) double pointed knitting needles and 4 ply Loopy Legends cast on 72 sts …24,24,24. Join into a ring being careful not to twist the stitches.
Work 4 rounds of K1, P1 rib.
Continue in stocking stitch working from

graph from right to left until all 31 rounds have been worked.

Work a further 31 rounds K1, P1 rib.

Decrease Round – * K1, P1, 8 times K2tog, rep from * to end of round…68 sts.

Heel – Slip 10 sts from end of second needle on to the beginning of the third needle, these 32 sts are for the heels.

Turn the knitting inside out.

Divide the rem sts between two needles and leave for the instep.

Note – Heel is worked in one of the contrast colors. Choose color of choice.

1st row – *Sl 1, Knit to end.

2nd row – Sl 1, Purl to end.

Rep these two rows a further 14 times.

Turn heel – K19, Sl 1, K1, psso, K1, turn, P8, P2tog, P1, turn, K9, Sl 1, K1, psso, K1, turn, P10, P2tog, P1, turn, K11, Sl 1, K1, psso, K1, turn, cont in this manner until all sts are worked onto one needle and 20 sts rem. Knit back 10 sts. Heel is now complete. Slip all instep sts back on to one needle. Take one needle and knit 10 heel sts, pick up and knit 17 sts along side of heel. With another needle knit across instep sts. With another needle pick up and knit 17 sts along other side of heel, knit rem 10 heel sts. Knitting is now back in the round. Work one round dec 2 sts evenly on needle two.

Shape instep

1st round – Knit.

2nd round – First needle – Knit to last 4 sts, K2tog, K2; Second needle – Knit; Third needle – K2, Sl 1, K1 psso. Knit to end.

Rep these two rounds until 17 sts rem on needle one and three and 34 sts rem on needle two.

Knit one round.

Work the first 6 rounds of the graph again.

Continue without further shaping until foot measures 14cm (5½in) from where sts were picked up at side of heel (or length desired).

Shape Toe

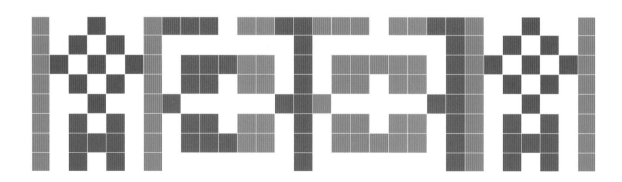

Note – Toe is worked in one of the contrast colors – choose color of choice.

1st round – Knit.

2nd round – First needle – Knit to last 4 sts, K2tog, K2; Second needle – K2, Sl 1, K1, psso, knit to last 4 sts, K2tog, K2; Third needle – K2, Sl 1, K1 psso, Knit to end.

Rep these 2 rounds until 8 sts rem on needle one and three and 16 sts rem on needle two. Knit one round and then first needle of next round. Slip sts from third needle on to end of first needle thus completing the round.

Toe is now ready for grafting (refer to page 12 for instructions). Darn in all ends. Press lightly if needed.

Make another sock to match, using a different contrast for the heel and the toe.

87

VALENTINE HEARTS

These socks feature a border of hearts around the top of the leg and a patterned heel featuring rows of little hearts. Knitted in a beautiful royal purple, rich dark pink and with a contrasting cream toe I think they are a beautifully romantic sock, but naturally you could make them in any color you like. Remember when knitting with two colors be careful not to pull the second color too tightly across the back of the work.

SKILL LEVEL
Advanced knitting skills

SIZE
Ladies small to medium foot (UK 5–8, EUR 37–42, US 7.5–10.5)

TENSION
38 sts and 44 rows to 10cm (4in) of stocking st using 2.25mm (UK 13, US 1) double pointed knitting needles.

Please measure tension carefully. If fewer sts try using one size smaller needles. If more sts, try using one size larger needles.

MATERIALS
Yarn:
- 1 x 100 g (3½ oz) ball of 4 ply, Royal Purple sock yarn.
- 1x 50 g (2 oz) ball of 4 ply, Cream sock yarn (Contrast A).

- 1 x 50 g (2 oz) ball of 4 ply, Deep Pink sock yarn (Contrast B).

Note – you will not need all the pink and cream yarn.

Knitting Needles:
- 1 set of 4, 2.25mm (UK 13, US 1) double pointed knitting needles.
- Wool needle for grafting toe and darning in ends

Socks
(Make 2)
Using the double pointed knitting needles and 4 ply Purple cast on 72 sts…24,24,24.
Work in K2, P2 rib for 7.5cm (3in).
Change to stock st and work Chart A, working each round from right to left.
Continue in stocking st in Purple 4 ply until work measures 19.5cm (7¾in) from cast on edge.

Dec round – *K16, K2, rep from * to end of round, 68 sts.

Work a further 2 rounds st st.

Divide for heel – K16, slip last 16 sts from needle three on to same needle. Divide rem sts between two needles and leave for instep.

Note – Heel is worked backwards and forwards commencing with a purl row.

Commence Chart B – using contrast B for the little hearts. Work 3 repeats of the 10 row chart. Work 1 row purl using Purple 4 ply. Break off contrast.

Turn heel

K19, Sl 1, K1, psso, K1, turn, P8, p2tog, P1, turn, K9, Sl 1, K1, psso, K1, turn. P10, P2tog, P1, turn, K11, Sl1, K1, psso, K1, turn. Cont in this manner until all sts have been worked on to one needle and 20 sts rem. Knit back first 10 sts.

Place all instep sts back on to one needle.

Shape Instep

Knit first 10 sts, pick up and knit 18 sts down first side of heel. With next needle knit instep sts. With next needle pick up and knit 18 sts along other side of heel knit rem 10 heel sts. Knitting is now back in the round.

1st round – Knit.

2nd round – First needle – Knit to last 4 sts, K2tog, K2; Second needle – Knit; Third needle – K2, Sl 1, K1, psso, Knit to end.

Rep these 2 rounds until 17 sts rem on needle one and three and 34 sts on needle two.

Cont without further shaping until foot measures 15cm (6in) from where sts were picked up from side of heel.

Shape Toe (change to Cream 4 ply)

1st round – Knit.

2nd round – First needle – Knit to last 4 sts, K2tog, K2; Second needle – K2, Sl 1, K1, psso, Kto last 4sts, K2tog, K2; Third needle, K2, Sl 1, K1, psso/ Knit to end.

Rep these 2 rounds until 7 sts rem on needle one and three and 14 sts on needle three. Knit one more round, finishing by knitting all the stitches from needle one on to needle three. Toe is now ready for grafting (refer to page 12 for instructions).

Chart A

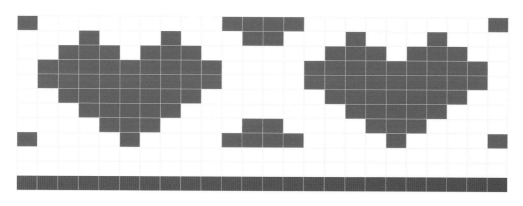

Number	Name	Strands	Estimated Lenght
DMC 5200	White Bright (B5200)	2	4.1 in.
DMC 3839	Lavender Blue MD	2	4.1 in.
DMC 3801	Christmas Red LT	2	17.1 in.

Chart B

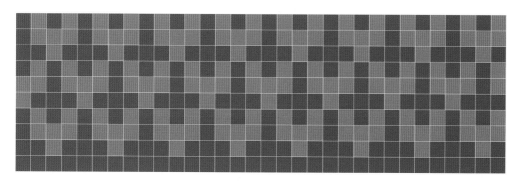

Number	Name	Strands	Estimated Lenght
DMC 3838	Lavender Blue DK	2	30.2 in.
DMC 603	Pink Mauve Med	2	24.7 in.

CARAMEL BOOT SOCKS

Winter weight men's 8 ply boot socks. These are great for the walker or the camper. Knitted in warm 8 ply with calf shaping they will be a standout amongst your men in the family. 8 ply socks are a great project to get started on knitting in the round on a set of 4 needles. The knitting is quicker than 4 ply and it is easier to maintain your tension.

SKILL LEVEL
Basic knitting skills

SIZE
Men's foot (UK 10, 11, 12; EUR 44.5, 46, 47; US 11, 12, 13)
Length – 30 cm (12in) to beginning of heel.

TENSION
25sts and 34 rows to 10cm (4in) in width measured over stocking st using 3.25mm (UK 10, US 3) double pointed knitting needles. Please check your tension carefully. If less sts try using one size smaller needles. If more sts try using one size larger needles.

   Note – The Ribbed top of the socks has been made using the main color for one sock and shade A for the second sock but there will be sufficient yarn to make both socks with the same tops if you desire.

MATERIALS
Yarn:
- 1 x 100 g (3½ oz) ball of 8 ply main color (Caramel)
- 1 x 50 g (2 oz) ball of 8 ply in 4 contrasting shades
  A - Dark Brown
  B - Mid Brown
  C - Cream Fleck
  D - Pumpkin

Knitting Needles:
- 1 set of 4, 3.25mm (UK 10, US 3) double pointed knitting needles
- Wool needle for grafting toe and darning in ends

Stripe Pattern – Stocking Stitch (every round knit)

2 rounds Main Color

2 rounds A

2 rounds B

2 rounds C

2 rounds D

Socks
(Make 2)

Using a set of 4, 3.25mm (UK 10, US 3) double pointed knitting needles and main color 8 ply, cast on 64 sts …22,20,22. Join into a ring being careful not to twist the stitches.

1st round – * K1tbl, P1, rep from * to end of round.

Rep this round until work measures 7.5cm (3in) from cast on edge.

Slip last st off first needle on to beg of second needle and first st of third needle on to end of second needle, 2,22,21 sts.

Commence Stripe pattern – Work in Stripe pattern until work measures 15cm (6in) from cast on edge.

Calf Shaping

Next round – **(Keep continuity of Stripe Patt correct)** – K1, K2tog, knit to last 3 sts, K1, Sl 1, psso.

Work 5 rounds Stripe patt.

Repeat these 6 rounds 3 times, 56 sts.

Continue in Stripe patt without further shaping until leg measures 30cm (12in) from cast on edge.

Begin Heel.

Note – Heel is worked backwards and forwards in rows on 2 needles in a solid color and the remainder of the stitches are held on 2 needles for the instep.

Next row – Knit the first 14 sts of round on to a needle, slip the last 14 sts of the round (needle 3) on to the same needle, 28 heel sts. Divide the rem sts between two needles and leave for the instep.

Using Shade D

1st row – Sl1, Purl to end.

2nd row – Sl 1, Knit to end.

Repeat these 2 rows a further 9 times and then first row once….21 heel rows.

Turn Heel – K17, K1, Sl 1, psso, K1, turn. P8, P2tog, P1, turn, K9, Sl 1, K1, psso, K1, turn, P10, P2tog, P1, turn, cont in this manner until all sts are worked on to one needle, 18 sts.

Knit back the first 9 sts (this completes the heel). Slip all the instep sts back on to one needle.

Note – Foot will be worked in main color Caramel and Toe in contrast color of choice.

Using first needle – Knit rem 9 heel sts and then pick up and knit 13 sts along side of heel; Second needle – Knit across instep sts; Third needle – Pick up and knit 13 sts along other side of heel, knit rem 9 heel sts. Knitting is now back in the round.

Shape Instep

1st round – Knit.

2nd round – First needle – Knit to last 4 sts, K2tog, K2; Second needle – Knit; Third needle – K2, Sl 1, K1, psso, Knit to end.

Repeat these two rounds until 14 sts rem on needle one and three and 28 sts rem on needle two.

Cont without further shaping until foot measures 17(18,19)cm (6¾(7,7½in) from where sts were picked up at side of heel.

Change Color For Toe

Shape Toe

1st round – Knit.

2nd round – First needle – Knit to last 4 sts, K2tog, K2; Second needle – K2, Sl 1, K1, psso, K to last 4sts, K2tog, K2; Third needle – K2, Sl 1, K1, psso, Knit to end.

Repeat these 2 rounds until 20 sts rem, 5 sts on needle one and three and 10 sts on needle two.

Knit one round and then first needle of next round. Slip sts from third needle on to end of first needle thus completing the round. Toe is now ready for grafting (refer to page 12 for instructions).

Make another sock to match, using a different contrast for the top ribbing and the toe.

LORNE

These calf length socks for men were made when I was on holiday in Lorne. Looking out the window at all the greens and browns of the trees there were sudden flashes of red from the wings of the crimson Rosellas, so hence these socks are named for that little week of peace and quiet. Lots of men don't want brightly colored socks but I think most men will love these well fitting, warm calf length socks.

SKILL LEVEL
Intermediate knitting skills

SIZE
Men's small to medium foot (UK 8–9, EUR 42–43, US 9–10)
Leg Length – 30cm (12in) to heel (can be lengthened)

TENSION
35 sts and 40 rows to 10cm (4in) in width over stocking st using 2.25mm (UK 13, US 1) double pointed knitting needles..
Measure tension carefully. If fewer sts try using one size smaller needles. If more sts, try using one size larger needles.

MATERIALS
Yarn:
- 1 x 100 g (3½ oz) ball of 4 ply, Trekking sock yarn Brown, multi

- 1 x 100 g (3½oz) ball 4 ply, Trekking sock yarn Red, multi (only a small amount will be used)

Knitting Needles:
- 1 set of 4, 2.25mm (UK 13, US 1) double pointed knitting needles.
- Wool needle fro grafting toe and darning in ends.

Mens Calf Length Socks
(Make 2)
Using set of 4, 2.25mm (UK 13, US 1) double pointed knitting needles and Brown 4 ply cast on 82 sts, 28,26,28. Join into a ring being careful not to twist sts.
Work in K1, P1 rib for 7cm (2¾in).
Change to stocking st and work 10 rounds (every round knit).
Join in Red 4 ply and work 10 rounds alternating 1 round Red, 1 round Brown.

Break off Red, and work a further 10 rounds Brown.

Commence Shaping for Calf

Next round –- K1, Sl 1, paso, Knit to last 3 sts, K2tog, K1– at the same time keep stripe pattern correct. Knit a further 5 round st st in stripe pattern.

Repeat the last 6 rounds until 66 sts rem.

Cont in st st without further shaping until work measures 24cm (9½in) from beginning of rib.

Divide for Heel

Knit first 17 sts of round on to one needle, slip last 17 sts of round on to other end of same needle, these 34 sts are for the heel. Divide rem sts between two needles and leave for instep.

Note – Heel is worked backwards and forwards in rows on two needles.

Work 29 rows stocking st on heel sts always slipping first st purl ways on a purl row and knit ways on a knit row.

Turn Heel – Knit 19, Sl 1, K1, psso, K1, turn, P8, P2tog, P1, K7, Sl 1, K1, psso, K1, turn, P8, P2tog, P1, K9, Sl 1, K1, psso, K1, turn. Cont in this manner until all sts are worked onto one needle and 20 sts rem. Knit back 10 sts, thus completing heel. Slip all instep sts back on to one needle.

Shape Instep and Foot

K10, pick up and knit 17 sts down side of heel. With next needle knit across instep sts. With next needle pick up and knit 17 sts along other side of heel, knit rem 10 sts.

Knitting is now back in the round.

1st round – Knit.

2nd round – First needle – Knit to last 4 sts, K2tog, K2; Second needle – Knit; Third needle – K2, Sl 1, K1, psso. Knit to end.

Rep these 2 rounds unto 17 sts rem on needle one and three and 34 sts on needle two.

Cont without further shaping until foot measures 16cm (6½in) from where sts were picked up from side of heel.

Shape Toe

1st round – Knit.

2nd round – First needle – Knit to last 4 sts, K2tog, K2; Second needle – K2, Sl 1, K1, psso, Knit to last 4sts, K2tog, K2; Third needle – K2, Sl 1, K1, psso. Knit to end.

Rep these 2 rounds until 8 sts rem on needle one and three and 16 sts on needle three. Knit one more round, finishing by knitting all the stitches from needle one on to needle three.

Toe is now ready for grafting (refer to page 12 for instructions).

MORNING MIST

Not all men want plain socks. Liven up the sock draw with this stripy pair. The variegated 4 ply yarn is shaded from aqua through to deep purple. These are a calf length pair with subtle shaping to ensure a good fit. The leg and foot length can be altered, you ill need extra yarn if you do want to make them longer. There will be plenty of the grey but not a lot extra of the variegated blue.

SKILL LEVEL
Intermediate knitting skills

SIZE
Men's small to medium foot (UK 8–9, EUR 42–43, US 9–10)
Leg length – 30cm (12in) to heel (can be lengthened)

TENSION
38 sts and 44 rows to 10cm (4in) of stocking st using 2.25mm (UK 13, US 1) double pointed knitting needles.
Measure tension carefully. If fewer sts try using one size smaller needles. If more sts, try using one size larger needles.

MATERIALS
Yarn:
- 1 x 100 g (3½ oz) ball of 4 ply, Poems variegated sock yarn in blue.
- 1 x 100 g (3½ oz) ball of 4 ply, medium grey sock yarn (note – entire amount will not be needed)

Knitting Needles:
- 1 set of 4, 2.25mm (UK 13, US 1) double pointed knitting needles.
- Wool needle for grafting

Socks
(Make 2)
Using a set of 4, 2.25mm (UK 13, US 1) double pointed knitting needles and 4 ply variegated Poems, cast on 72 sts, 24,24,24. Join into a ring being careful not to twist sts.
Work in K2, P2 rib for 6cm (2¼in).

Commence Stripe Pattern
Stripe pattern is as follows – 4 rounds of Blue variegated Poems, 4 rounds of 4 ply grey.
Work a total of 15 stripes altogether.

Commence Shaping for Calf

Next round – K1, Sl 1, paso, Knit to last 3 sts, K2tog, K1 – at same time keep stripe pattern correct. Knit a further 5 round st st in stripe pattern.

Repeat the last 6 rounds until 66 sts rem.

Cont in stripe pattern without further shaping until leg measures 30cm (12in) from cast on edge.

Divide for Heel

Note – heel is worked backwards and forward in rows on 2 needles using poems only and the remainder of the sts which are for the instep are held on the rem 2 needles.

Next – Knit the first 16 sts, slip the last 16 sts from needle three onto the same needle (these are the heel sts). Divide the remaining sts between 2 needles and leave for instep.

1st row – Sl 1, Purl to end.

2nd row – * Sl 1, K1, rep from * to last st, K1.

Rep these 2 rows 13 times and then 1st row once.

Turn Heel – Knit 21, turn, P10, turn, K9, Sl 1, K1, psso, K1, turn, P10, P2tog, P1, turn, K11, Sl 1, K1, psso, K1, turn, P12, P2tog, P1, turn, K13, Sl1, K1, psso, K1, turn P14, P2tog, P1. Cont in this manner until all sts are worked onto one needle, 20 sts.

Knit back 10 sts.

Place all instep sts back on to one needle.

Shape Instep and Foot

K10, pick up and knit 17 sts down side of heel. With next needle knit across instep sts. Next needle pick up and knit 17 sts along other side of heel, knit rem 10 sts.

Knitting is now back in the round.

1st round – Knit.

2nd round – First needle – Knit to last 4 sts, K2tog, K2; Second needle – Knit; Third needle, K2, Sl 1, K1, psso, Knit to end.

Rep these 2 rounds until 17 sts rem on needle one and three and 34 sts on needle two.

Cont without further shaping until foot measures 18cm (7in) from where sts were picked up from side of heel.

Shape Toe – (change to grey 4 ply)

1st round – Knit.

2nd round – First needle – Knit to last 4 sts, K2tog, K2; Second needle – K2, Sl 1, K1, psso, Knit to last 4 sts, K2tog, K2; Third needle, K2, Sl 1, K1, psso, Knit to end.

Rep these 2 rounds until 8 sts rem on needle one and three and 16 sts on needle three. Knit one more round, finishing by knitting all the stitches from needle one on to needle three.

Toe is now ready for grafting (refer to page 12 for instructions).

First published in 2016 by New Holland Publishers Pty Ltd
London • Sydney • Auckland

The Chandlery Unit 704 50 Westminster Bridge Road London SE1 7QY United Kingdom
1/66 Gibbes Street Chatswood NSW 2067 Australia
5/39 Woodside Ave Northcote, Auckland 0627 New Zealand

www.newhollandpublishers.com

A record of this book is held at the British Library and the National Library of Australia.

ISBN 9781742577098

Managing Director: Fiona Schultz
Publisher: Diane Ward
Project Editor: Holly Willsher
Designer: Lorena Susak
Production Director: Olga Dementiev
Photography: Samantha Mackie

Printer: Toppan Leefung Printing Limited

10 9 8 7 6 5 4 3 2 1

Keep up with New Holland Publishers on Facebook
www.facebook.com/NewHollandPublishers